Mindfulness Therapy

Six Ways to Achieve Real Happiness, True Knowledge and Inner Peace

(The Present Moment in a Constant State of Peace and Happiness)

Hector Larose

Published by Rob Miles

© **Hector Larose**

All Rights Reserved

Mindfulness Therapy: Six Ways to Achieve Real Happiness, True Knowledge and Inner Peace (The Present Moment in a Constant State of Peace and Happiness)

ISBN 978-1-989990-91-9

All rights reserved. No part of this guide may be reproduced in any form without permission in writing from the publisher except in the case of brief quotations embodied in critical articles or reviews.

LEGAL & DISCLAIMER

The information contained in this book is not designed to replace or take the place of any form of medicine or professional medical advice. The information in this book has been provided for educational and entertainment purposes only.

The information contained in this book has been compiled from sources deemed reliable, and it is accurate to the best of the Author's knowledge; however, the Author cannot guarantee its accuracy and validity and cannot be held liable for any errors or omissions. Changes are periodically made to this book. You must consult your doctor or get professional medical advice before using any of the suggested remedies, techniques, or information in this book.

Upon using the information contained in this book, you agree to hold harmless the Author from and against any damages, costs, and expenses, including any legal fees potentially resulting from the application of any of the information provided by this guide. This disclaimer applies to any damages or injury caused by the use and application, whether directly or indirectly, of any advice or information presented, whether for breach of contract, tort, negligence, personal injury, criminal intent, or under any other cause of action.

You agree to accept all risks of using the information presented inside this book. You need to consult a professional medical practitioner in order to ensure you are both able and healthy enough to participate in this program.

Table of Contents

INTRODUCTION 1

CHAPTER 1: TURBO BOOST YOUR IMMUNE SYSTEM 3

CHAPTER 2: WHY PRACTICING MEDITATION? 10

CHAPTER 3: BUILDING MINDFULNESS HABITS 25

CHAPTER 4: PHYSICAL & MENTAL EFFECTS OF STRESS 45

CHAPTER 5: PAYING ATTENTION TO OUR 5 GIFTS 52

CHAPTER 6: MINDFULNESS IS… 58

CHAPTER 7: MINDFULNESS IS A PRACTICE 65

CHAPTER 8: EXERCISES IN BREATHING AND RELAXATION 70

CHAPTER 9: CONQUER THE FEARS AND WORRIES 80

CHAPTER 10: NATURE OBSERVATION 89

CHAPTER 11: WHY STOPPED ENJOYING 93

CHAPTER 12: HOW CAN MINDFULNESS BENEFIT YOU? ... 96

CHAPTER 13: WHAT YOU PRACTICE GROWS STRONGER 103

CHAPTER 14: THE BIGGEST OBSTACLE TO MINDFULNBESS 107

CHAPTER 15: HOW DOES MINDFULNESS TRAINING BENEFIT US? 109

CHAPTER 16: WALKING MINDFULNESS 114

CHAPTER 17: HOW MINDFULNESS MEDITATION CAN CHANGE YOUR LIFE 118

CHAPTER 18: ZAZEN BREATH AWARENESS MEDITATION 123

CHAPTER 19: BEFORE YOU GET STARTED 134

CHAPTER 20: RECOGNIZING STRESS IN THE BODY 142

CHAPTER 21: THE BODY SCAN TECHNIQUE 156

CHAPTER 22: A MINDFUL BODY 161

CHAPTER 23: THE HEALTH BENEFITS OF MINDFULNESS. 178

CONCLUSION 182

Introduction

First of all, remember that to meditate you don't have to do anything special. Most people get confused on how to actually approach these techniques, because they believe they must "do something complicated", in order to reach a deep level of mental peace. In reality, just following my voice will be enough for you to dive deeper into your consciousness and relieve yourself from anxiety and stress.

Second of all, feel free to move during the practice if you are feeling uncomfortable. Trying to stay still in a position that does not allow you to relax will be detrimental to the meditation. Make any adjustment you deem necessary, moving will not affect your meditation session.

The meditations presented in this book are intended to tackle three different needs you may have. As the title suggests, the big 3 topics presented are sleep, anxiety relief and self healing. This is why each of the three practices is designed for a specific and defined reason. Nonetheless, each technique works well for every one of the three needs, as meditation cannot be seen and experienced without a wholistic approach.

Before each meditation, I will tell you some little details and interesting information about it and give you an insight on which of the three areas it primarily works on.

Chapter 1: Turbo Boost Your Immune System

As you explore and learn about mindfulness, you will realize the many ways mindfulness can benefit you. Your immune system can be strengthened, and your overall physical well-being improved. Making mindfulness a normal part of your everyday routine is fairly easy to do, and it is likely you will experience a noticeable improvement to your immune system.

How are mindfulness techniques beneficial to the immune system?

One of the key components of a strong immune system is reducing stress levels. Put another way, excessive stress is destructive to the health of your immune system. You will find mindfulness strategies are very effective at managing stress, therefore helping to keep your immune system functioning well. It is important to use the mindfulness techniques regularly and consistently. As you will learn, there is more than one mindfulness technique. You can use the method that you feel works most effectively for you.

Is the immune system optimized in other ways from mindfulness training?

One benefit of mindfulness is that you become much more in tune with your body. As you learn to eliminate distractions and effectively use mindfulness techniques, you will find yourself truly becoming one with your body. When something is out of balance, or you are becoming ill, you will quickly recognize the signs.

One theory of why mindfulness techniques help optimize the immune system is that the immune system is able to react immediately, fending off illness before it becomes full-blown. You will become aware of signs your body sends you warning you that you are becoming ill, such as aches and pains, a fever, or even a sore throat.

It is well-documented that a positive mental state directly results in a stronger immune system. By using mindfulness techniques, a positive collateral effect is the higher functioning immune system. When you feel stress, worry, or concern, your emotional state has a negative effect on your immune system, and the downward spiral can even contribute to depression.

Learning mindfulness techniques like meditation not only stimulate the immune system portions of your brain, they also help your body to produce antibodies, your body's defense system. Again, the effects of mindfulness training are cumulative, and you must consistently practice mindfulness in order to achieve these extraordinary benefits.

Why is a strong immune system necessary?

A strong, functioning immune system reduces stress levels and is able to fight off illness and infection. When you feel better, you have more energy. When you have more energy, it is normal to feel more positive about everything, and easier to handle minor frustrations or inconveniences. There is a sequence of positive effects with a strong immune system. Instead of being susceptible to illness, experiencing anxiety, and then becoming sick as you might with a weakened immune system, an optimized immune system will keep you healthier, prevent illness, loss of work due to illness, and when you have more energy, you feel better about yourself physically and mentally.

Optimizing your immune system using mindfulness techniques, as well as other healthy living patterns, is even more important during the flu season. Undoubtedly you will be exposed to colds and the flu, but a boosted immune system and a calm, stress-free outlook can prevent you from becoming ill. Remaining healthy is a great way to retain your energy, instead of feeling tired, worn down, and defeated, like you do when you have the flu.

What mindfulness technique is best to use to successfully optimize the immune system?

There is not really a "best" technique to optimize the immune system. All forms of mindfulness training can effectively focus you, and help you boost your immune system. Perhaps the best technique is the one you are most likely to stick to, devoting at least ten minutes per day every day to your mindfulness practice.

Variations of mindfulness techniques may be used to increase your immune system. In addition, use mindfulness training in the location most convenient for you. You may prefer to use mindfulness meditation outdoors, or in your car, or in your favorite room. It is important to practice daily, but the location of your mindfulness training is up to you. Mindfulness techniques used in nature settings are particularly effective mood and attitude-boosters. Experiment periodically to see what benefits you.

Can mindfulness meditation be done sporadically, or is consistency key to effectiveness?

You probably already realize the answer to this. Consistency is key to actually achieving and maximizing your results with mindfulness techniques. You will want to devote a minimum of ten minutes every day to mindfulness training. Practicing more than once daily nets even greater immune system benefits. It may take some time for you to realize you are achieving results, because it often takes eight weeks or so for the impact on your immune system to be noticeable. Practicing in a quiet spot or a tranquil area outdoors also boosts your results. Mindfulness techniques are beneficial to your body, your well-being, and your state of mind, so making the time to engage in mindfulness training is really a very positive investment in yourself that will pay you great dividends.

Chapter 2: Why Practicing Meditation?

Well, after reading all that, you should want to practice it just to see how it works and to get those benefits. But we'll explain a bit more about it here. Meditation bestows a host of benefits on its practitioner from the very first. Some are fairly obvious, like increased awareness of one's own mind and body. Others are often touted but sometimes not clearly explained, like relief from anxiety, depression, panic attacks and other mental illnesses. Perhaps this is due to a hesitance to accept non-western medicinal approaches to these things, though they are growing in popularity as healing skills, with both the medical community and the world at large. Meditation can also increase your energy and focus, help you change your behaviors, and improve your quality of work and exercise. It can even improve your immunity and overall health.

What Effect Does It Have on Your Brain?

Not only does meditation help you focus on the right stuff, but it makes your thought patterns faster, stronger, and more in your control. The 'fight of flight' response is the reaction most of us have to a stressful situation. In the past it was very useful, for example if we see a Tiger, we don't have time to think about it, we just need to run. And in the past, this fight or flight response was critical for keeping us alive. But today? Well, there aren't many tigers roaming the streets, and the worlds a lot safer in general. Most of us don't experience danger every day. However, most of us sadly use the same fight or flight response when they experience petty, pointless stress like road rage or arriving late to work. We've somehow managed to evolve to the point where we get stressed on an emotional and physical level, by things that really don't matter and don't affect our chances of survival at all. Things that really shouldn't have any effect on our emotional state and certainly not on our physical bodies and systems.

Remember, the fight or flight response has its place. If you're in a street fight or there's a natural disaster, yes you need that response. You need to be able to react, and move fast in order to protect yourself from harm. And it will be there for you when you need it. But most of us are reacting to an angry boss at work in the same way physically that we'd react to a vicious bear attacking us! The same hormones, stress responses, chemicals and processes are happening in our bodies in this situation! This means our bodies are experiencing more stress than ever before, because we've lost touch with our ability to be in our bodies and not our Minds. By being so focused on our minds, and our thoughts, we've lost the ability to be in our bodies. If we were in our bodies, your angry boss wouldn't matter at all. You'd probably laugh at how angry they're getting; I know I sometimes do! It's almost silly how angry people get at seemingly pointless or insignificant things.

Result of Stress on Our Body

When you experience the fight or flight response, your body pumps hormones like adrenaline and epinephrine through your veins. Your lungs expand and take in more oxygen and if you perceive the stress the still be there after a few seconds, you get even more. It's like a gas pedal being held down while the car isn't moving. After a while it burns the engine out, so now imagine the effect of that gas pedal being held down in your body for years on end. It's not good, I'll tell you that for free. It's actually very bad for your body and mind and over time, it can make you sick. And it does! Chronic stress, which is stress experience in little amounts over a long period of time can make your immune system weaker. Think about this the next time you're angry at someone cutting in front of you in traffic. By getting angry, you're literally making yourself ill.

It's quite funny to think about this. We're one of the most intelligent species (apparently) on the planet, and we for some reason choose to make ourselves ill and stressed because someone cut in front of us in traffic for a split second. It's crazy. We've become blind to what we're doing. Or, we'll get angry if the waiter brings us the wrong food by accident. This is how we actually behave in the world today! We choose to experience this stress, and it IS a choice. when you learn about meditation, and once you've read this book, you'll have the choice of how to react to situations like that. The fight or flight response interestingly, uses that same 'default mode network' It involves the amygdala, and produces hormones that flood your body with rage, energy and so on. It's useful for an actual fight or a situation in which you need to sprint to get away from danger. But it's pointless, and actually harmful to have that same response when your boss shouts at you, you're late for work, or the waiter brings you chips instead of soup.

So, the fight of flight response is not needed for 99% of our lives. We certainly don't need those stress hormones pumping through our body and not being used to run. It's very harmful. So, specifically, mindfulness meditation can actually shrink the part of your brain responsible for 'fight or flight' responses, which tend to be more emotional and not thought through. While it also strengthens your higher brain functions which happen in the frontal pre-cortex. This means you're more able to think on a higher level about things logically and reasonably. This means our normal responses to stress that we can't seem to control, are completely different. We're able, after just 8 weeks of meditation, to have much greater control over our thoughts and emotions in times of stress.

And this really works, I've managed to avoid almost all stress in my life for the years I've been meditating. And the great thing about that is that I've barely needed the stress response at all. My brain notices the oncoming bike before I've really realized what's happening consciously. A distress signal gets sent to my amygdala (in the default mode network, remember?). The amygdala works out that I'm in danger, and instantly sends a distress signal to my hypothalamus. That area of the brain is sort of like a command or control room. It decides how to act and it does all of this in tiny fractions of a second. It's incredible. This means the hormones remain in their system, and they stay amped up with high blood pressure and so on. Maybe you've experienced a situation where you're so annoyed, angry and stressed that you just can't sit still. You feel it flowing through your veins, right?

That's the hormones your brain is telling your body to give you, because it thinks you're in danger! It thinks you're about to have a fight or run for your life and it's supplying you with these hormones to give you energy. But if you don't use them or need them, the effect they have on your body is very harmful. To be honest, you probably have some idea that it's not a good thing to stay all jumped up and energetic for so long, right? Anyway, meditation helps you reduce that, so that you only get those stress hormones when you really need the to save your life. You won't catch me getting worked up over a meal that's late, or somebody cutting me off in traffic. It just won't happen because I value my health and mental and emotional state way more than that.

But there are other things meditation does to your brain as well. It can actually help you experience less pain. How? In the brains of advanced meditators, the pain centers of the brain actually light up more, but the people report feeling less pain. How can that be? It's a paradox, but it seems that meditation somehow helps people experience less pain. It does this in a very complex way. The way it works, is that mediators have actually decoupled (weakened) the link between the anterior cingulate cortex (area of the brain responsible for unpleasantness of pain) and the prefrontal cortex. That means they still feel the pain but it's much less.

The effect of pain in most people, in largely in the mind. There is some nervous system pain which is unavoidable, but the rest of the 'pain experience' we've all come to know is made up in the brain. It's a response to the real pain, and it can make it up to 10 times worse.

In a lot of people, there is a loop which means you constantly re-experience the same pain. But in meditators, this loop is mainly closed down. They're still aware of the pain, but it's much less than non-meditators. Amazingly, this effect can be seen even when people aren't meditating, meaning the meditation has caused a permanent change in their brain and the way they experience pain. This also applies to the lowered stress response. It seems meditation can physically change the brain for the better in just a few weeks. Now imagine having meditated for decades. It's no wonder that Buddhist monks are able to focus for days on end, seemingly be immune to pain, and even have control over their entire immune system and the intricate processes in their bodies. I don't know if you've seen the videos of the devoted Buddhist monks able to channel pain and strength around their bodies. One such video showed a monk resisting a sharpened spear to the throat simply by the power of intention and meditation. Now that's taken years to get to that point, but not everyone can get there.

Meditation Health Benefits

As described before, there are so many ways in which meditation improves mental health. It can assist in treating mental illnesses like depression and generalized anxiety disorder. Additionally, it can ease the chronic stress and distractibility most modern people struggle to master. Focus at work increases, and relationships with others improve. It allows you to build better connections and really listen and care what someone's saying. In short, meditation allows one to be relaxed, present, patient, and grow in wisdom and faith. Mindlessness, stress and anxiety are shown to damage the immune system and slow the recovery of injuries. They also slow the progress of weight loss, strength training and learning. A mind at peace is a mind capable of just about anything. Working to practice mindfulness pays huge dividends. Here are just a few other things you'll experience:

Better Sleep

Meditators are able to sleep better and relax deeper. This can lead to all sorts of interesting effects, like lucid dreams (being able to control the dreams and decide what to dream about) and decreased nightmares.

Improved Focus

Of course, one of the biggest benefits of meditation is being able to focus on things for long periods of time, and at an intense level. This is massively helpful if you're trying to achieve something or anything in your life.

Increases Grey Matter

The brains of meditators are shown to actually have more grey matter. Grey matter is like the bond that holds the brain together, and helps it fire signals and process information. The greyer matter you have, the faster and better your brain operates.

Helps You Get Into Flow State

Have you ever been writing something and you just get into the 'zone'? Or maybe you've been playing a sport of working out and you just get into that headspace that's unshakable and unstoppable. You're working faster, better, and more focused, and you don't notice the time passing? That's 'flow state' and meditation helps you get there more easily and more often.

Reduced Risk of Disease

This is actually something I want to explain a bit more about. Meditation has the ability to lengthen what are known as 'telomeres' making you resistant to all sorts of diseases like Cancer and Alzheimer's! Telomeres are like the 'protective caps' on the end of your chromosomes. But wait, what's a chromosome? A chromosome is essentially a thread of protein and DNA found in the nucleus of our cells. It's pretty important. On the ends of our chromosomes are telomeres. A telomere is like the protective plastic cap on the end of a shoe lace. It stops it fraying and going all horrible. So, telomeres stop our chromosomes getting stuck together and fraying, so to speak.

Over time though, our telomeres (protective ends of our chromosomes) get shorter. This means that sooner or later, our chromosomes are no longer protected and are not able to divide or heal themselves any more. This leads to the cell dying, mutating (cancers) or changing. And this is how ageing happens, our telomeres become shorter and shorter to the point where they can't effectively protect our chromosomes any more. So, our cells start dying. This is the natural ageing process, but it can be slowed down massively by meditating. Meditating actually lengthens your telomeres, meaning your chromosomes are much more protected for longer. Years longer. It's like giving your individual cells a suit of armor to protect them against the passing of time, and all you need to do for that, is to sit down and do nothing for ten minutes a day! Still sound like too much effort?

This means less cells die or mutate, so you look and feel younger. But it's not just about feeling younger though. When telomeres get too short and the DNA is left exposed, it can mutate or fuse to other things. Things that it shouldn't fuse to. They can become damaged. It gets dangerous, because it can actually cause things like Cancer and other diseases. So, there are a number of things that meditation can help you with. It can lengthen telomeres and make you more resistant to things like Cancer and ageing. It does this by increasing telomerase activity, which helps lengthen the telomeres attached to your DNA. Powerful stuff. But more than all of those benefits, comes the feeling of feeling better! Just feeling good in everyday life, and not having to worry about the stress's life or the negative aspects of life. It makes you feel good, and for a lot of people that's the most important thing. The increased focus, better sleep and immunity come as a bonus.

Chapter 3: Building Mindfulness Habits

Being mindful is an innate ability that resides within us all. The only reason **why** we're not doing it as often as we should is because we're so consumed by everything that is happening around us that we have forgotten how to utilize this skill to our advantage. We've forgotten what it means to be present and connect with our mind and body. The beauty of mindfulness is what an easy practice it to adopt. You don't need to make any major life changes. You don't need to alter your beliefs and principles. You don't even need to turn your life around entirely to begin reaping the benefits of mindfulness.

All you need is to start training yourself to be more aware of **everything** that you do. Ponder this quick question for a moment:

How many things do you do in a day on autopilot?

Probably a lot of things, if not nearly everything. We're so busy rushing from one thing to the next that we rush through the motions too. Anything that we can do in a hurry we will and the stress of trying to juggle it all becomes part of the package. The term "mind"-fulness would suggest that this practice is beneficial only for the mind, but research conducted in recent years reveals that it is just as beneficial for the body. Studies to date even indicate that mindfulness has a role to play in several aspects of our physical health.

The 7 Benefits of Mindfulness for Your Body

One body. That is all you're going to get in this lifetime. That's all **everyone** is going to get. One life, one body, one mind, heart, and soul. If you don't cherish the body that you have and take care of it the way it deserves, it won't be long before your body starts to break down gradually. You won't even feel it at first or realize that it is happening until it's too late to do anything about it. Your body is the vehicle that you are going to journey through life with, and you **must** take care of it both on the inside and out for better health physically, emotionally, and mentally.

Mindfulness is one of the many ways in which you will come to realize what your body needs and what it does not, and it certainly **does not need** the stress that you put it through every day. Actively practicing mindfulness brings awareness to just how much your body is affected by stress, especially when it manifests itself as physical pain. We've covered some of the basic reasons why mindfulness is good for you in general, but now let's focus on what it can do specifically for your body.

Bringing awareness to the way that your body feels through each experience will help you forge a closer connection to your body in a way that you never have before. By frequently "scanning" your body for an overall assessment of how you feel, you start to notice all the little things that you missed before you began practicing mindfulness. You notice every itch, every ache, and every tingle even in the smallest parts of your body. You notice when you start to feel any pain in your body, you notice when you feel cold, warm, pleasantly comfortable, and more. All of the sensations that you feel will always be accompanied by some emotion or thought, and it is through mindfulness that you start to **listen** to what your body is trying to tell you.

• **Benefit #1 - Possible Slowdown of Aging Cells.** Who wouldn't want to look younger if they could? The beauty industry is a booming business for one simple reason. We're always on the lookout for the proverbial fountain of youth. Anything that holds the promise of turning back the clock and reversing the signs of aging gives us a little bit of hope. Yet, the easiest way to slow down the signs of aging, as it turns out, could be to practice mindfulness to minimize stress. Cell aging is a natural occurrence, but it is sped up by stress, unhealthy lifestyle choices and the diseases we contract. Some studies suggest that those who practice long-term mindfulness meditation could potentially have greater telomere lengths. Telomeres are a protein that is at the end of the chromosomes in our bodies. This protein is the one responsible for protecting our chromosomes from the signs of aging, and it would seem mindfulness has a positive impact on this. A research review in 2018 showed links between mindfulness training and increased telomere activity, which could suggest that mindfulness is working in this domain. That would explain why some scientists appear to be optimistic that mindfulness could be the anti-aging fountain of youth we've been searching high and low for all along.

• **Benefit #2 - Better Heart Health.** It's no secret that heart disease is one of the leading causes of death, especially in the United States with one in four deaths annually attributed to this condition. Given that heart disease is associated with chronic stress levels, mindfulness is the way towards better heart health, given the circumstances. In a study that was conducted on participants who were dealing with pre-hypertension, those who learned how to meditate mindfully showed significantly greater improvements in their diastolic and systolic blood pressure levels. This was in comparison to other participants who were given an augmented drug as their treatment instead of a mindfulness program. This suggests that mindfulness could have an important role to play in lowering the risk of high blood pressure and the associated heart conditions that go along with it. Yet another study that was conducted revealed that participants who chose to undergo a mindfulness program had a significant improvement in their 6-minute walking test that measured their cardiovascular capacity. The American Heart Association also published their review which concluded that the evidence was adequate to suggest that there were benefits to making mindfulness an adjunct treatment for the prevention and treatment of coronary diseases.

- **Benefit #3 - A Healthy Pathway to Weight Management.** Weight gain or weight loss are some of the many symptoms associated with excessive stress. Yet, we brush it off and don't think twice about the connection between these symptoms and stress. We don't realize how this behavior pattern and way of thinking of is having damaging effects on our health. When you're preoccupied with stress, there are two ways you could react to it. One, you'll eat in excess as a coping mechanism to feel better, which will result in weight gain. Two, the stress you feel could be so intense that you lose your appetite entirely. Neither approach is healthy and without mindfulness, it's going to be hard to break out of this destructive cycle. Living in a world today that is designed for convenience certainly isn't helping matters, with fast food and deep-fried unhealthy options available around every corner. The only way to put a stop to it is through mindful awareness. To realize why you feel the way you do, what's causing it, how you're reacting towards it, and what you need to do to put a stop to it.

• **Benefit #4 - Promotes Better Sleep.** It is amazing what a good night's sleep can do for you. Yet, struggling with insomnia and poor, restless sleep at night is becoming an all too common phenomenon these days. Especially when our minds are riddled with worries. How many times have you found yourself lying in bed awake at night, tossing and turning as you tried to get some sleep yet all you could think about was how stressed you feel? Every day, our lives present us with new challenges. Every day, we try to find a balance between managing our careers, families, relationships, finances, health, and wellbeing. By the time the end of the day approaches, you feel so exhausted, drained of energy that you go through the motions without connecting with the world around you. Excessive worry is going to have both long and short-term effects on your wellbeing. Not getting enough sleep will affect your ability to make decisions, rob you of happiness, aggravate any physical medical conditions you already have which are often associated with high levels of stress. You need mindfulness for better sleep at night, it will do your body a world of good.

- **Benefit #5 - Greater Resilience Physically and Mentally.** Mindfulness is about bettering yourself overall, and it encompasses several aspects that go beyond learning how to control your thoughts. One of these aspects involves building resilience both mentally and physically to overcome the obstacles and challenges that are thrown your way. There are only two ways to achieve the goals you set for yourself - one is to set them, two is to achieve them. Most of the time when we give up and feel physically unable to push forward anymore, it is often because our mind has given up first. Without resilience, the desire to give up can be too overwhelming to reject. Setbacks, failures, disappointments along the way, feeling like every time you take one step forward you take two steps back, that is enough to wear you down and can diminish the desire that you have to keep on pushing forward. When stress becomes a byproduct of these emotions, your body starts to feel defeated as the symptoms begin manifesting physically in the form of aches, pains, and muscular tension. It won't be long before you eventually give up altogether because it does not seem worth it to keep going anymore.

• **Benefit #6 - Coping Mechanism for Depression.** Depression is one of the most debilitating mental conditions that a person can experience. Depression robs you of joy and makes life feel like it is a constant struggle. Feelings of despair, hopelessness, and unhappiness that cannot be explained threaten to drown you in what may seem to be a never-ending cycle of misery. Some days you don't even feel like you have the energy to get out of bed because depression can be so overwhelming. Sometimes it feels like there is nothing that can help you, and it is exactly why you need mindfulness. It has been used for centuries to achieve mental well-being and happiness, satisfaction, emotional stability. When combined with mindfulness meditation, it reduces and minimizes the risk of experiencing depression by limiting the production of excess cortisol in your body, which has been known to be the cause of many stress-related disorders, depression included. Both mindfulness and meditation are effective in helping you balance the neurotransmitters in your brain, especially dopamine and serotonin which have been strongly linked to causing depression.

- **Benefit #7 - It Allows Greater Control Over Your Emotions.** Our emotions are sensitive to what is happening around us. When you're stressed, you're emotional. Emotions can get the best of you when you don't know how to control them. This is why learning to deliberately slow down your thoughts and emotions can go a long way towards helping you learn how to exercise greater self-regulation over your actions. Being emotional can make it difficult to keep a clear head and you react based on your impulses instead. Mindfulness helps you stay in control every step of the way, so you are the one

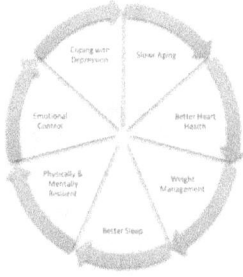

who remains in the driver's seat always.

7 Benefits of Mindfulness

Mindfulness In 5-Minutes

Mindfulness is advocated as one of the best stress management tools out there, and for good reason too. You only need 5-minutes of mindfulness to take control of your life again and start reducing worry, stress, anxiety, and any other negative emotion you may be battling with. 5-minutes of your day is all it takes to begin cultivating this life-changing, positive habit. If you live a high-stress life for whatever reason, you **need** this skill in your life to help you cope with stress before it starts to weigh you down.

Anytime you need think you need a quick 5-minutes to center your thoughts and calm yourself down, step away from what you may be doing at that moment and practice the following exercise:

• **Step 1:** Find a comfortable, quiet space where you can be alone for the next 5-minutes. You can either choose to sit or stand during this process.

• **Step 2:** Close your eyes for maximum focus.

• **Step 3:** Take a deep breath, inhaling deeply while you make a conscious effort to relax your body. Nothing should feel stiff or tense as you focus on the breath that you draw in while simultaneously thinking about how your body feels.

• **Step 4:** Let your mind start to focus on how your body feels, pay attention to it. Notice its position, what it feels like, and relax while you breathe in and out in concentrated, controlled breaths.

• **Step 5:** - Next, start to really hone in on your breathing. Notice the air flowing in and out. Empty your mind of all thoughts except the act of breathing.

That's it. That is all that you need to do for the next 5-minutes. Occasionally, you will notice your mind start to wander and when you do, bring it back to your breathing again. It's okay if your thoughts drift, maintaining focus requires practice. The focal point of this exercise should be to allow yourself to feel more relaxed with each breath you take. To pay attention to **everything** from the way your body is positioned, to the sounds you may be hearing around you.

You can continue the exercise for longer than 5-minutes if you have more time on your hands. But for those who have a busy day lined up ahead and you don't have the time for a lengthy mindfulness session, it is still possible to see the change even if you only have 5-minutes to spare. The power of mindful is truly incredible, and it is something that you need to experience for yourself to believe. The sense of fulfillment, peace, and well-being, along with all the other benefits mentioned above is a testament to how powerful this simple, yet effective technique to overcome worry can be.

Other Mindfulness Building Exercises When You "Don't Have Time"

So much to do, yet so little time to do it. That's one thought we all have at least once, if not several times throughout any given week. It's part of the reason why we're so high strung and up to our eyeballs in stress. You've probably heard of mindfulness before you even started this book but then thought to yourself you barely have enough time as it is, so piling something else unto your already full plate feels like you're asking for trouble. Until now when it has finally dawned on you that mindfulness **isn't going to take up much time at all.** Not in the least.

When you're feeling pressed for time, you've got the 5-minute workout above that you can do anytime, anywhere once you've found a quiet space to do it. Should you feel like you need other exercises to practice when you **can't** find a quiet spot, try one of the mental exercises below:

Quick Mindfulness Exercise 1 - Enhancing Awareness

Since the theme of mindfulness is all about becoming more of your body, your mind, and your thoughts, this exercise is going to focus on exactly that. Sharpening your focus to remain alert to not just your surroundings, but your thoughts as well. For example, if you were mindfully aware of your thoughts, you will have better control when it comes to keeping any negative thoughts or emotions at bay, right?

This exercise is going to enhance your awareness both internally and externally. Beginners often find focusing on awareness to be a struggle in the beginning, because it's so easy to let our thoughts drift and get distracted by everything else. Take your time, there's no need to rush through the process.

• **Step 1** - Begin by choosing an activity or an object to focus on. Pick something that you would normally do without thinking twice about it, like opening the door or getting dressed in the morning.

• **Step 2** - Once you've got your object or activity, start to really, actively pay attention to what you're doing. If you're opening the door, concentrate on it. Reach for the doorknob and be aware of how it feels in your hand, and the motion of pulling the door towards you or away from you. Stop and appreciate how lucky you are to be healthy and fit enough to walk out your front door with a destination and a purpose in mind. If your chosen activity is to be mindfully aware as you get dressed in the morning, focus on what you're doing instead of just going through the motions. Concentrate on how the fabric of your clothes feel in your hand, and even stop to appreciate how fortunate you are to be able to have a selection of clothes to choose from as you go through

your closet looking for something to wear.

Quick Mindfulness Exercise 2 - Enhancing Mental Focus

Successful mindfulness requires the ability to concentrate and not let your thoughts get easily distracted. Which means you're going to need to work on improving your focus. Luckily, the exercise is simple enough and once again, easily done anywhere, anytime.

• **Step 1** - Pick an object to focus on and place it in front of you.

• **Step 2** - When you're ready, set a timer and start to focus on the object and nothing else (this is the same kind of concentration you need to exercise each time you are actively mindful).

• **Step 3** - Concentrate on that object and keep staring at it for as long as you can. When your mind begins to wander, stop, and make a note of how long you managed to concentrate on that object before your mind started to drift.

Gradually, you should be able to focus on the object in front of you for longer periods before you find yourself getting distracted. The longer you can focus on the object, the better your ability to focus will become. Eventually, maintaining mindfulness for a prolonged period is easily doable.

Chapter 4: Physical & Mental Effects Of Stress

Effects Of Stress

Regardless of the source of the stress, if it is chronic and left untreated, it can affect you physically, mentally, spiritually, and emotionally. You will feel consistently tired and irritable, and you may even start to get headaches.

There is no direct physical relationship between stress and your health, but there is definitely an indirect one. Stress can definitely have an effect on your physical, mental, and spiritual health and could actually have a part in you becoming ill.

Change is not easy, and it takes much practice and lots of affirmations. It can sometimes seem difficult to change, but once again, it's all an illusion, as we said!

You can be anything that you imagine yourself to be, and those who live an effective lifestyle are well aware of the power that they have to change or reframe any situation. Stress can have a very negative effect on your health and overall life.

When you feel like you are stuck and having a problem moving past something that you have been through, try starting something brand new. This will give you something else to occupy your time, and you will not focus on how bad you feel.

It can and will play a large part in your body, having negative reactions to the fact that you stay constantly in a stressful state of mind. Most patients who visit their doctor have ailments due to many stress-related issues.

Stress is the way that your body responds to something that it may perceive to be harmful to you. When a threat is perceived, you will experience a chemical reaction that will enact an automatic defensive response that is intended to prevent you from getting sick or contracting a disease.

These are a few ways that stress can affect you on the physical level:

Stress can cause you to have headaches, have muscle pains, chest pains, nausea, insomnia, anxiety, helplessness, and extreme depression. In addition to causing physical pains and tensions, it can cause you to be really tired, demotivated, uninterested in having sex, and feeling angry all of the time.

It can cause you to feel completely overwhelmed and really withdrawn from others.

This usually leads to constant insomnia, feeling the urge to medicate with alcohol or drugs, wanting to be alone and isolated from most people.

Physical Effects Of Stress

Can and will increase your blood pressure

Hypertension

Cardiovascular disease

Extra blood sugar

Reproductive Chronic stress

Impotence

Arthritis

The situations and pressures that cause stress are most commonly called stressors. Most of us normally look at stressors as being something negative, which they can be. When you work too much, are involved in a toxic or abusive relationship, do not eat well, and never get any exercise, most likely, you are really stressed out.

Just because you may not be aware of the stress, that does not mean the stress is not present within you. When life demands too much of your time and energy, this can cause you high amounts of stress. When you anticipate negativity or an outcome that is not going to go well, this can also cause stress upon yourself, because you are taking time to worry about something that may not even happen.

Finally, your perception of what is happening can also cause you to be stressed, because you may perceive something totally different than what is actually going on. Something that you may think is difficult in your relationship might be something that can be worked out with a simple conversation that you have been avoiding because you anticipated an argument.

Your sense of control, your self-confidence, and the belief you have in yourself, may all be affected by stress if you do not get a handle on it quickly. It can demotivate you and get you off of the positive and successful road that you have been traveling on.

Your ability to deal with your emotions will completely disappear if you are not aware of how to get yourself back into a calm state and relax when you get upset. This will only add to the level of stress that you may already be dealing with and cause you to become more withdrawn and depressed. You are no longer optimistic, positive, motivated, or inspired. You become isolated from everyone, and because of that, your depression becomes worse than it ever has been.

This is all because people choose not to address the fact that they are stressed and tend to think that it is not as serious as it actually is. It will eventually lead you to engage in more and more negative self-talk, excessive drug and alcohol abuse, being totally unrealistic, and finally damaging important relationships.

Eventually, you will begin to feel helpless, hopeless, and very negative towards anyone who you come into contact with during your everyday life. The way that you think will also be affected, because you no longer look for the good, you start to only be able to see the bad or negative and you also predict negative outcomes as well.

Your attention span, memory, and the way we deal with emotions can all be impacted by long-term stress, and it can also lead to both physical and mental illness through effects on the heart, immune and metabolic functions, and hormones acting on the brain.

Some of the emotional and behavioral symptoms of stress overlap with those of mental health conditions like anxiety or depression. Chronic stress increases the risk of developing depression and anxiety in some people. The precise mechanisms of how stress is linked to mental ill-health are being uncovered.

Chapter 5: Paying Attention to Our 5 Gifts

Very often in life, over the course of a long period of time growing up, whether we are in school or at home, we were taught to pay attention to our surroundings, observe what other people do, things and examples were pointed out to us for us to list out all the "don't do" and "must do" in life in order to be a "good person" or "do good and well" in life. At which point of time in your life were you taught to pay attention to yourself? By that I really mean pay close attention to the point where you know yourself inside out.

Down to the smallest and seemingly absurd details that no one knows, or able to know–but you. Have you ever stopped to observe the way your breath falls fast and slow along with your heart beat each time you are excited or scared, noticed how the pores on your skin opens and closes up each time you are freezing cold or enduring the blistering heat, you see water pouring out of them to keep you cool and so your body temperature remains stable?

How many times a day have you thanked yourself for the amazing physical body you were "gifted" with since the day you were born? How the cells in your body knows exactly where to go and reside inside that intelligent "shell" to best serve you and keep it in perfect balance and harmony? Did you know each time you think a negative thought, you disrupt the entire system and make it work harder than it has to work for?

Your body was designed in a way to make you function well enough to compete, to play, to work and every single one of you instrumentally was born to have that potential. Your thoughts are the culprit for the dis-eases in your body accumulated over weeks, months, even decades for some. You blame it on the weather, on your fate that you resigned to, as "life as it is". How many times have you caught yourself saying, "It is what it is", and you think that you have no control over it?

We were born with "gifts" for us to enjoy the minute we came into this world and breathed our first air. If we are one of the lucky ones to "have it all" and have our 5 senses intact, we have the ability to see; to taste; to hear; to feel; to smell. How often do you maximize that gift and stretch it to its fullest ability, and "do good with it"?

Do you find yourself at one point in life experimenting and testing its limits and abusing it with substances and come across really unpleasant experiences with these "gifts" that were given to you with the purpose of enjoying life? Imagine the amount of pleasure you can milk from these simple 5 gifts that are working for you day and night, and it never stops for anything else in this world, but you. The way you choose, and the way you decide to use them, it is the only thing you know for sure that works in your favor, if you choose wisely, with the best in-tent.

If you choose to watch the news on the TV broadcasting violence and killings, hear gossips, negative comments about people when they gather in their specific groups, choose to smell cigarettes and take in second-hand smoke into your lungs, choose to taste and feel the kind of foods you pick and put into your body to feed your mind and soul. All these choices, no one else made them but you.

Day in and out, we make the choices ourselves and we abuse these basic senses and "abilities" that were given to us but thinking the "world outside" is the one making a living hell out of our lives. It gives us nothing else but endless opportunities to enjoy the simple pleasures anytime we want, every time we want it. We just got to line up with the decision to intentionally use them wisely.

What exactly does it mean to feel alive? Heightened. You do every possible thing to make sure your senses are heightened in the right way. You elevate your senses in a positive manner and you feel light and you feel happy. You feel alive. It really is as simple as that. You choose carefully before you look at it, listen to it, taste it, touch it, and take a whiff of it.

That decision itself will do you much justice, or at least gets half the battle won already. You "open up" new eyes for yourself to appreciate the beauty of nature around you, look at the people you live with or co-create with, be in a state of appreciation and love and you come to enjoy all sorts of wonderful conversations, music, and taste all kinds of wonderful foods that will nourish not only your body, but your mind, and it feeds your soul. You will come to touch people in ways that are beyond your wildest imagination. You will literally touch their hearts when you choose kindness and gratitude every day.

These, your senses, are the small details that are the "big things" or at least will create the "big events" for yourself, brick by brick, layers on top of layers. That is where you lay the foundation of practicing self-awareness. If you don't even know your "self", who else in this world can do it for you?

Chapter 6: Mindfulness Is…

After learning about how powerful mindfulness can be in your life, you are probably wondering what it is exactly and how you can achieve this state. You may be wondering exactly how mindfulness can add all that value to your life, and what it takes to get there. After all, inner peace is what we are all looking for, isn't it?

Mindfulness is a state of consciousness, if you are looking for the most basic definition. However, if you want to get deeper into it, the practice of mindfulness means you are paying attention "on purpose". You are purposefully and consciously directing your awareness, instead of allowing your awareness to ride on "autopilot". It is important to realize that mindfulness and awareness are two separate words, and that although they are often interchanged, they are actually two separate things. It is best if you learn to separate them now and that you do not get into the habit of using these words interchangeably.

Self-awareness involves a vague awareness of your current state from moment to moment. For example, you may be aware that you are feeling angry. However, that is not the same as being mindful about your anger. If you were being mindful about your anger, you would be purposefully aware of the anger, meaning that you would notice every element of it. Instead of just realizing you were angry, you would realize every element of your anger and how it was affecting you. You would recognize what is happening around you that is triggering this anger, and you would recognize the internal state that it is bringing up.

Let's take a look at the practice of drinking tea to further explore what mindfulness is and how you can be mindful. Imagine you are drinking a tea in the midafternoon. At this time, you are likely also thinking about what is on the television, something you heard about earlier today, and several other things all at the same time as you are drinking your tea. You may be aware of the tea, and you may even be aware of the unique flavor, but you are not being mindful about the experience of drinking the tea. In this circumstance, you are likely only vaguely aware of your experience of drinking the tea in your cup, and potentially some of the sensations involved. It is likely, however, that you are not aware of the thoughts and emotions attached with that beverage.

This occurs because, in our natural state, we are only vaguely aware of our thoughts as they occur. Our thoughts often wander about from thought to thought in an unrestricted manner. When we are being mindful, though, our thoughts will remain on what we are doing in the present moment. We will be less focused on what happened in the past or what we expect to or hope will happen in the future and more focused on what is happening in the present moment. We will think about the situation we are in, the environment around us, the feelings we are having, and all of the senses that are being awakened and used throughout the experience.

The part of mindfulness that is the most important part is the purposefulness of it. When you are living with the purpose of staying in the same space as your present moment, whether you are staying in tune with a particular emotion or physical experience, this means that you are actively taking control over your mind and shaping it with your own intention.

"Mindfulness isn't difficult; we just need to remember to do it."
-Sharon Salzberg

When it is left to its own devices, your mind will take the time to wander through all sorts of thoughts. These thoughts express all different types of emotions from sadness, anger, revenge, depression, happiness, joy and otherwise. The more that you allow yourself to indulge in these thoughts, the more you reinforce those emotions within' your own heart and cause yourself to suffer. The majority of the time when we are suffering from our thoughts, we are remembering events that happened in the past that caused painful emotions in us. It is important that we take the time to realize that the past is over and no longer exists. The only moment that we can actually experience is the present moment, and this seems to be the one that we often do our best to avoid, usually through thoughts and emotions.

As you can see, mindfulness is purposefully being present in the moment and noticing exactly what is happening right now, not before and not after. Knowing this, it doesn't mean that we cannot think about the past or the future. However, when we do, we should ensure that we are doing so from a mindful state of consciousness that allows us to stay aware that we are not currently existing in that time and the only moment we have is the present. Therefore, we can choose how we will consciously allow for that experience to change us or affect us.

There are many ways that you can learn to become present in the moment. Later in this book, you will learn about practical methods to achieving mindfulness. These tools are a great way for you to successfully exit an emotionally charged state of mind that may be causing you to suffer and will allow for you to use your state of consciousness to grow. When you purposefully direct your awareness, you are able to "anchor" yourself in the present experience and decrease the effect that certain thoughts and emotions can have on your life. Instead, you will be able to create a space of freedom where you can allow calmness and contentment to grow.

Chapter Summary:

- Mindfulness is a state of peace, not necessarily happiness
- Self-Awareness and mindfulness are two

different things
- Mindfulness is being purposefully aware of yourself
- Our mind wanders if we don't consciously choose our thoughts
- Mindfulness is being present in the moment you're in
- You can still think about the past and future, just do so mindfully

Chapter 7: Mindfulness is a practice

Now comes the hard part. I know you're in a hurry. I know you really don't have the luxury of time, but if you wish to benefit from mindfulness you have to understand that it is a practice. It is something that you have to do. It's something that you have to implement on a regular basis. Otherwise, the benefits won't be as even as you would've hoped. Here are just some considerations to keep in mind regarding your mindfulness practice.

Doing it consistently is better than erratic practice

I'm not at all claiming that you will not benefit from a sporadic mindfulness practice. I'm not saying that at all. If you are particularly sensitive, even if you engage in mindfulness once a week, it's not impossible for you to feel less stressed and more in control over your life.

With that said, the probability of that happening is quite lower than if you engage in mindfulness practice consistently. The good news is that you don't have to put in a huge amount of time. You don't have to block out ridiculous chunks of your precious daily time for mindfulness to work for you.

You only need to invest as little as 15 minutes or so for mindfulness to work for you. In fact, even if you have less than 10 minutes, it could still work for you as long as you use a minute-by-minute approach, which I will outline in this book.

Duration is not a deal killer

There's no need for you to feel bad if you can't devote hours to a mindfulness practice. There's no need for that. By simply choosing to be consistent with your mindfulness practice, you will enjoy its benefits. In fact, if you play your cards right, the less time you need to invest in mindfulness as you practice more. You expend less time, but you would still get the same level of results. Isn't that awesome? It should be because like I said before most people don't have the luxury of time.

Don't get thrown off by "the best" form of mindfulness

When you look at Google search terms for mindfulness topics, one of the most common search phrases people use is "the best mindfulness". I'm telling you right now, there is no such thing.

The reason why this is the case is because "the best" is subjective. What may be the best for you, with your own particular set of circumstances, might be completely horrible to somebody else, because guess what, their set of circumstances is completely different.

So instead of getting all hung up about what is the best way to engage in mindfulness or what is the best form of mindfulness, focus instead on identifying a practice that best fits your particular situation. Everybody's got different needs.

Everybody comes from different backgrounds. We all have different experiences that we bring to the table. We have different preferences.

To think that there is some sort of magical one-size-fits-all solution that would apply across the board to all people regardless of their differences is simple wishful thinking. Don't fall for hyped claims that assume that there is such a thing as the best mindfulness solution. Get that idea out of your head. Such a solution doesn't exist.

The better approach would be to look at the different flavors of mindfulness that I will outline below so you can come up with an informed choice as to which way to go. Of course, the best approach would be to try them all out and pick the method that works for you based on your experience.

Of course, even if you've identified a method doesn't mean that it will work perfectly. What this cherry-picking process will enable you to do is to pick something that has the highest likelihood of working and then tweaking it and fine-tuning it so it produces the best results.

Chapter 8: Exercises in Breathing and Relaxation

In this chapter, I want to prepare you for mindfulness. It's not something that comes naturally to you, especially if you are accustomed to living in modern times and have found that your job stresses you and you find that it's hard to keep up with your financial commitments. You may already be suffering from stress or anxiety because of the life that you live. The reason why preparation is needed is because you won't be accustomed to:

- Stillness of the mind

- Breathing in the correct way

Stillness isn't forced. It is something that happens when you learn to let go of all the worldly worries and no one could expect you to jump from your hectic life into being able to do this without some form of preparation. Thus, that's what this chapter is all about. We are going to have a little fun with mindfulness to get you ready for the real thing.

To show you how undisciplined your mind is, I want you to put aside half an hour for this first exercise. What I need you to do is to be away from distractions. Now, start to breathe and try to consciously think of nothing for as long as you can manage it. Take a note of this because it will help you to see the progress that you have made during your initiation into mindfulness. Breathe, avoid thought. Breathe, avoid thought. You won't last long and I want to explain why. During the course of our days, we tend to hone in on things that have happened and things that bugged us or that stayed in our minds. We have this impression that our thoughts should be given priority. Let me give you an example. When Elizabeth Gilbert was asked to try this, as shown in her book "Eat, Pray, Love" she couldn't still her mind. She had recently broken up with her husband, but she considered that the marriage was important enough a memory to hold onto and not let go of. It was almost as if her thoughts for her failed marriage gave it some kind of validity in her mind. Of course, when you learned what a nonsense that was and did eventually let go, she was able to feel the benefit, but I merely used this example to show you why we hoard thoughts.

This small exercise should show you that there's not much you can do at this time to let go of thoughts. However, you can channel your thoughts in a much more constructive way. First you need to learn how to relax and breathe correctly, so this chapter is all about preparation for mindfulness, rather than mindfulness itself.

Learning to relax

For this exercise, I need you to be dressed in something that is comfortable. Tight waist bands or uncomfortable clothes will distract you because over the course of the exercise, your attention is drawn to the discomfort, rather than concentrating on what needs to be done. You need to lie down on the bed and use one pillow – even if you are accustomed to using two. This allows your head to be in the right position for you to breathe correctly because your airway is free.

Now, close your eyes. If you need to cut out light, draw the curtains, but when you are relaxing, you need as little distraction as you can get and the harsh light from outside may interrupt you even if you have your eyes closed. The idea of the exercise is to think of each body part in turn and then tense that part of the body before relaxing and allowing that part of your body to totally relax. Feel it get heavier and then move on to the next part of the body. Let me show you what I mean.

Close your eyes and imagine your toes. Tense your toes. Breathe normally, and while you are breathing let the toes relax. When the toes are relaxed, move on to the soles of the feet and do the same thing. Tense the area and then allow it to relax. The body parts that you will relax will be as follows:

- **Toes,**
- Soles of feet
- **Ankles**
- Calf area
- **Knees**
- Thighs
- **Waist**
- **Stomach**
- Chest or breast area
- **Shoulders**
- Upper arms
- Lower arms
- **Wrists**
- **Knuckles**
- **Fingers**

When you have been through these, you can also include your shoulders, your neck and the different areas of the face.

While you are doing this, your blood pressure will go down and your heartbeat will slow. This is normal, so don't try getting up too fast after you have finished the relaxation process. Instead of doing that, simply examine how you feel and take a note of it. This is not mindfulness, but it helps you to get a lot of the stresses out of your system so that you are more capable of getting into mindfulness easily.

Breathing

When you breathe in an everyday situation, you usually only use about a third of your lung capacity. This is normal but when you use mindfulness, the idea is to use all of your senses and practicing breathing in a deeper way will help in many ways. Inside your body, you have something called the sympathetic nervous system. You don't need to know all that it does, but when you breathe deeply, the oxygen from your breathing is able to be distributed to all the right places in the body because of this nervous system.

Something that helps you with your breathing is to sit upright with your back completely straight. This allows energy to go through your spine to what are known as chakras, or energy points. Your posture is very important in all exercises because if you block off these energy points, you may find that you do not benefit fully from the exercises. Be mindful about the straightness of your back. If you can choose a dining chair which gives you support, place your feet flat on the floor and do not lean back.

Now start to breathe. For the inward breath, breathe through the nostrils to the count of eight. Hold the breath inside you for a moment and then breathe out to the count of ten. The reason for the exhalation being longer than the inhalation is that you are trying to expel all stale air from your system and replace it with fresh air. Counting is quite important in another way too. While you are counting the length of your breaths, you are less likely to divert your attention to other things, so it's a great thing to practice for your mindfulness sessions.

Do you remember feeling panicked at some time? The reason you feel this kind of panic is because you take in too much oxygen and over-oxygenate. That's why people who are stressed are asked to breathe into a paper bag to lower the level of oxygen in order to lessen the stress on the body. When you learn to breathe properly, you are able to use this at any time of day or night to help you to be present in the moment and to be able to escape all of those stresses that stop you from relaxing.

If you want to check if you are doing this correctly, place one hand flat against the upper gut while you breathe and you should feel that hand move as you breathe in a kind of pivoting motion. Usually you don't breathe that deeply, but it's always a good thing to spend a little time breathing like this because it helps you also with your mindfulness meditation which is all part of what mindfulness is all about.

Learn to simply be

In this exercise you learn acceptance of this moment. Try to sit still for a moment within your day and just let go of all thoughts. Observe the way you breathe and observe the things around you. This is something that is very efficient when you perform it in a natural environment because you can enjoy all the elements of nature and this is something that's fun. Too often we forget to observe what's around us and nature can bring us back to reality in the nicest possible way.

If you need to relax and you need to give your brain a little bit of space from the stress of the day, this is a very good exercise to help you to drop things that really don't matter in the order of things. If someone upsets you, they only upset you because of the way you judge the message of whatever they said to you. This relaxation lets you let go. It will take a while before you learn not to judge, but when you do, you will find it very useful indeed because it frees you from the shackles of judgement and believe me, you are more shackled than the person who gets under your skin. Let go. Enjoy something natural and simply observe it. It will refresh you and make you feel better about life. The sooner you can drop negative energy, the better.

Several times during the course of the day, stop your life and hold the moment because when you do that, you find that there is so much in your life that will otherwise be missed. It may be in the flicker of light from an autumnal sky. Inspiration may come from the opening up of a rose bud, but if your mind is too busy with the future and worries that you refuse to let go of, you will miss that great experience and will never be able to recapture it.

Chapter 9: Conquer the Fears and Worries

Give it a thought and be amazed at the fact that your story is the same as of Mark Twain. It is hard, even for the bravest of men, to avoid worries and fears about the unknown misfortunes. The man has this wonderful ability to associate with the events which have nothing to do with him. This ability creates fear, and this is the fear which keeps our mind busy in thinking about.

Every day, we hear about people dying, accidents, hardships, and unfortunate blast victims. These events have an immense impact on the mind, and we start imagining such events happening to us or our beloved ones. Can we get rid of such worries? Yes, of course, but for that, we again require mindfulness cultivation.

Worries and Anxiety

Anxiety is the result of three distinct mental characteristics:

1. Cognitive
2. Behavioral
3. Psychological

There are various symptoms of anxiety, observable in our body such as a swift heartbeat, fatigue, clammy hands and tension in the muscles. These occur due to the psychological impact of anxiety. The cognitive aspect triggers the feeling of fear and worry. It triggers fearful thoughts. The psychological aspect is related to the practical part because behavioral aspects force us to avoid certain activities in anticipation of getting away with the events we are worried about.

The problem with our thinking activity is that most of the time it visualizes the wrong events. We start worrying so much that we prepare ourselves for such worries.

Are you thinking the solution? The solution itself is mindfulness. As we have already learned that mindfulnesses are about concentrating on the present, there will be less room for the mind to think about the worries. But it is not as simple as you may think. The problem is, our mind triggers fear when it observes something happening to someone else, which watching news, reading a newspaper or going through online news. This is the stage when an event rises as a reality, and as we have trained our brain to focus, it focuses on unfortunate events as well. So, now to this point, our focus must be on restricting our mind from associating ourselves with the real victims of the sad events.

In this regard, one thing is important to realize that everything is not for everything. Whenever a bad thing or event happens, we must realize that there are millions of those, who did not suffer from that event in other words, why worry about something which never happened to your or what never happened to millions of others.

Please, make sure avoid carelessness but at the same time maintain the balance by not worrying about the things which are not under your control. If somebody died in an accident, shall you avoid driving a car? Let me be frank! If scores of people die in an earthquake strike, will you quit living in the population and reside in an open place of a jungle?

What is the solution then?

There is only one working solution which is "Be Brave and Have Faith." You have to realize that if something bad is going to happen it will, and you cannot paralyze your life in an attempt to remain safe. The best approach is to be brave and continue with your normal life. Don't be careless but don't become a patient. The feelings of fear generate quickly, but they fade away quickly as well. But you need to engage yourself in the present activities to let the fear escape from your mind. Do you believe that one day you'll die? Well, the answer is obviously a YES. Now, compare the fear of death with some other fear. How many times a month do you remind yourself of death? And what is the intensity of that fear? Death is a harsh reality, but we don't feel this fear too often because our thoughts are engaged with scores of fears linked with our lives.

We need to understand that our fears are because of our unnecessary focus on the adverse events. We fear more about day to day failures and mishaps. So, we need to guide our mind to shift the focus.

People suggest that optimism is a good option, but there is one problem with optimism. Limited optimism is not an issue but if optimism goes beyond limits (fantasy), we ought to be disappointed in the end. There is only one way to fight against fears and worries, and I describe in a single word "IGNORE."

Let us go back to the starting lines of this chapter, borrowed from Mark Twain. He is true because we develop fear in our imagination. Everything in life doesn't go wrong, but fears keep us stuck and a point comes when we realize that we just wasted too much of our time and energy.

By the time we realize this fact, normally it gets too late.

Our lives are wasted because of imaginative fears. We need to focus on our present circumstances and work hard enough to keep things right. Just keep reminding yourself of the responsibilities. You need to engage yourself. For this, a simple routine can work for you:

- Set small targets, monthly or bimonthly

- Keep track of your daily activities

- Write down your responsibilities and then check every day whether you fulfilled the responsibilities or not

- Don't forget to include pleasure times in your weekly schedule

- Pleasure times could be, outing to a park, visiting friends or family members, inviting friends or family members

This is a simple yet effective routine. The advantage of this routine is that your life will be disciplined, it'll keep you engaged, and you will focus on improving your life.

When you focus on your short-term goals and achieve these goals, you enable yourself to convince your mind about a bright future and positive events.

Pleasure times are essential for this routine to work well. During the weekends, if you stay in bed and avoid physical activities, spend time watching the TV or in front of the laptop, there are chances that your imagination will pick up something fearful. This is why pleasure time means spending a good time in the company of the people you love and admire. This communication will keep your mind fresh and happy. There is another advantage of pleasure times. Throughout the first five days of the week, you'll wait for the weekend your mind will anticipate good communication, simples, joys and everything positive. In this way, worries and fears will stay away from your mind.

Seeing the Light in the Dark Aspects

Life is cruel in a sense that the rise and fall is the part of it. Happy times; no issues, but bad times; we feel scattered. By avoiding worries and fears, we can remain happy and satisfied with the present situation but it doesn't stop anything wrong if it is to happen anyway. There is a need to be brave and strong enough to face bad situations. For this, we need have faith in the fact that bad times are followed by good times and good times are followed by bad times. There is no escape, but we can avoid mental stress by accepting the challenges. Remember, mindfulness is about being aware of the present and accepting it. If, presently, you are facing a bad event, be aware of it and accept it but never accept the defeat. Do your best to deal with it gracefully.

You have to convince your mind, throughout good or bad times, that it is the part of the life cycle and it happens to all 6 billion people in the world. Bad times are your test, and these are the times when you can verify your abilities. It is an opportunity to demonstrate the power of your character. Take it as a bright opportunity to show others what you really are, how hard you can fight and how gracefully you can come up with the solutions. Believe me; there is no joy more significant than the one you experience after bravely dealing with a critical situation. Nothing is permanent in this world so are the situations. It is our test, as a human being, and the outcome could be used as the grading scale of our character and personality.

In Chapter 3 we'll discuss the role of mindfulness in dealing with our relationships. Life is not about ME, it is about the US, being a community, being a family and being a colleague so we can never ignore the importance of respect for the relationships.

Chapter 10: Nature Observation

Most of us also have the habit of neglecting the things we commonly see every day. In our way to work, for instance, rarely do we stop and look at the beautiful scenery in our surroundings.

To become more aware or mindful of our surroundings, you should train your mind to observe the things going on around you actively.

In one of your downtimes for instance, you can sit in a nearby park and find a place where you can sit down comfortably.

You should set your timer for 2 minutes. In the given time, you should keep your attention focused only in one object, preferably, something not man-made.

While sitting surrounded by nature, you should pick a tree, a bush or an animal and observe its details. When observing a tree for example, you should observe how it moves when the wind passes by. You should also observe its branches and leaves. You just look at it without thinking too much.

When we see something that we are familiar with, we often bring out past learnings related to the things we are looking at. When you observe the tree, you may be tempted to think about the information you have learned back in biology class. You may think about how the tree grows. You may also develop questions in your mind regarding the tree.

You should avoid entertaining these thoughts if you want to achieve the state of mindfulness. This task will be difficult for people who are used to creating patterns of information in their minds. However, they are also the ones who are in most need of this mindfulness exercise.

You should look and observe your selected natural object without creating judgments about that object or pulling out knowledge learned in the past.

You should keep your mind focused on that object until your timer sounds. This may seem easy but most people who are stressed out will not be able to do it for 2 minutes.

The more stressed you are, the more uneasy you feel when you sit down and do this exercise. Most people living a busy lifestyle cannot take sitting down and just do nothing. Their minds immediately become occupied with thoughts about their goals or the things they are stressed about.

When your thoughts begin to take your attention away from your tasks, you could breathe deeply 3-5 times before forcing your mind to go back to the task at hand.

This activity is meant to train your mind to focus even in things that you are not interested in. Some of the tasks that we need to do are uninteresting to us and we show our lack of interest in our behavior. When talking to someone who is uninteresting for example, most people tend to take out their phones. They multitask their communication.

This not only leads to a bad first impression from strangers but also affect your relationships with your loved ones. By taking your time to observe the small details without passing judgment, you will train yourself to be better at focusing on the things that truly matter to you.

CHAPTER 11: WHY STOPPED ENJOYING

Add chapteWhy Did You Stop ?

It is because we are conditioned only to enjoy and feel happy when we come first in class or any given Task or when we feel we better than someone or better than our previous self i.e what you were Yesterday, Tomorrow or months early. In One word answer to kill enjoyment is COMPARISONS.tring to become somebody or self in the past you lose your identity But oh I have heard this before I know this tell me something new. if this is what comes to mind then you are a slave to your ego. Its called relative happiness or enjoyment, its good sometimes in down periods of life to lift ourselves up, its relative like swinging pendulum. Happy-sad-happy-sad

All work and no play - where is the fun in living that way? First is the suggestion that you write down the activities you do in a typical day

and mark whether they nourish or deplete you. This can be a bit of an eye opener. For example I have spending time on Face book and walking my kids to school. My first instinct is to say the walk to school depletes me because it is physical hard for me and leaves me in some pain and facebook nourishes me because it is a leisure activity.
But then I think about it for a while and realize that actually face book often depletes me. Seeing unhappy, boastful or intentionally aggressive status updates and stories leaves me feeling dissatisfied with my looks, life, friend choices etc. Walking the girls to school is an important part of their day and mine. Yes it is painful but I am mindful of the need to keep mobile and this is a positive choice I am making. I get to see the trees, flowers and hear birds. I often walk with a very good friend of mine and always feel brighter for our talks whatever the subject. I miss the walk when my husband is at home and I don't do it. The walk is nourishing. The purpose of the activity is

understanding how much of our life is devoted to depleting not nourishing is the first step in redressing the balance - learning to dance again enjoy again.
Fun Practices for 7days
Carry out 3 mindful techniques of your choice this week mentioned ahead. Chose one that you feel gave you appreciable nourishing benefits and choose one that you feel you didn't get fully to grips with the first time and add in breathing spaces a couple of times a day and also use that practice to ground you whenever you feel stressed. Use the breathing space and then afterwards consider what action you can take to deal with the source of stress.

Chapter 12: How Can Mindfulness Benefit You?

It's a busy old life for most of us. You try to fold up your laundry while watching the kids and the television or the cooker at the same time. You may plan out your day while you are on the way to work or while getting breakfast in the morning and then you might find time to plan your weekend as well. Sadly, while you rush about trying to keep up with tasks that just have to be done, you find yourself losing the connection with the here and now, missing out on exactly what you are doing and how you are feeling. How many of us can honestly say that we noticed whether we felt rested when we woke up or if we just got out of bed and started our day on automatic pilot? Did you actually smell the coffee you were drinking this morning or notice that the forsythia has finally bloomed this morning while you were on the way to work?

Probably not and that is where mindfulness meditation comes in. Mindfulness is all about learning to focus on the present and accept it without criticism or judgment.

Mindfulness is rooted in Buddhism but nearly every religion will include some kind of meditation or prayer that will help you to stop focusing on what you can't change in the future and concentrate on the present, on cultivating an appreciation for life as it happens. Even though it could be argued that the academic and scientific research on mindfulness isn't as deep-seated as that on, let's say, diet and exercise, there is a very good reason why it has been in existence and in use for thousands of years. Gradually we are starting to understand more and more about mindfulness and how it affects every aspect of our lives.

I am going to tell you 11 good reasons why you should incorporate mindfulness meditation into your life on a daily basis.

It Lowers Stress Levels

Recent research has shown that, not only can mindfulness help you to feel less stressed, it is actually linked to a lower level of cortisone, the stress hormone that our bodies produce. It isn't just a feeling; it is reality – it truly does lower stress levels.

You Get to Know the Real You

Mindfulness can let you see beyond the rose-tinted glasses, especially when you really need to analyze yourself objectively. A study that was published in the Psychological Science journal showed that, through mindfulness meditation, you could learn to get over blind spots that stop you from seeing your own flaws.

It Can Help Arthritis Sufferers to Handle Stress Better

Recent studies have shown that, while mindfulness may not be able to relieve pain in sufferers of rheumatoid arthritis, it can help to reduce their levels of fatigue and stress that, in turn, make pain management much easier.

It Can Help You Even When You Are Not Practicing

Once you have learned the art of mindfulness, you don't actually need to meditate for it to benefit you. Studies have shown that the amygdala, the region of the brain that responds to emotional stimuli, is changed through meditation and this effect will happen even if you are not actively meditating at the time.

Mindfulness Has Four Helpful Elements

One of the true benefits of mindfulness meditation is that it contains four elements that help us in different ways – body awareness, regulation of attention, regulation of emotion and self-awareness. All of these help you in different areas of your life and your health, whether singly or together.

It Can Make You a Nicer Person

While mindful meditation helps you personally, it also helps the people around you in beneficial ways. People who meditate and practice mindfulness on a regular basis are far nicer people to know and are more likely to do good for others.

It Can Help Cancer Sufferers

Mindfulness meditation has been shown, paired up with art therapy, to be beneficial in reducing the symptoms of stress in women with breast cancer. The study was carried out at the Jefferson-Myrna Brinda Center of Integrative Medicine and imaging tests done alongside the study showed that mindfulness is linked with changes in the brain relating to stress, reward, and emotion.

It Can Help You to Fight Off Colds and Flu

As well as practicing a good hygiene regime, mindfulness meditation, paired with exercise, can help to reduce the effects of nasty colds and flu. Research done at the University of Wisconsin School of Medicine and Health showed that those who practiced mindfulness missed fewer days of work from illness, such as acute respiratory infection and also found that the colds were not so long in duration and were not so severe.

It Can Lower the Risk of Depression Amongst Teens and Pregnant Women

Teens who are taught the art of mindfulness meditation at school can have a lower risk of stress, depression, and anxiety. Also, 25% of pregnant women are at risk of depression but practicing mindfulness yoga can help to reduce that risk significantly.

It Can Help You to Lose Weight

No, it isn't a quick weight loss fix but mindfulness can help you to reach your goals by reducing the stress that goes with trying to lose weight and teaching you to see your goals more clearly and get over or tackle any negative emotions that stand in your way.

It Can Help You to Get a Better Night's Sleep

According to research at the University of Utah, mindfulness practice helps you to control your emotions better along with your moods and that can lead to a better night's sleep. Those who practiced mindfulness regular found that their brain was less active at night because they had less stress and worry and that meant sleep came easier and was more restful.

The next step, now that you know how mindfulness can help you, is to learn how to do it. Let's move on to the next chapter.

Chapter 13: What you Practice Grows Stronger

When you practice mindfulness in a daily routine, what you find is that it awakens senses that you may not have used for a while. For example, how often do you make a cup of coffee and savor the aroma. Of course, people do in the adverts because they are trying to sell you a product but most people don't even taste their cup of coffee. It is merely drunk automatically while we are on the go. This is a missed opportunity. When you practice mindfulness, you can apply it to any activity that you wish to participate in.

Mindful Conversations

These are conversations where you listen more than you usually do. Often you miss the pointers that people want you to catch because you only listen superficially. Have you ever said, "How are you?" to someone and then walked away before they had a chance to answer? The fact is, we all do this, but we miss the opportunity to learn because we are too busy living our lives. Phone someone. Be aware of listening and you will learn that mindfulness helps you to be more compassionate.

Mindful eating

When you sit down to eat your food, look at everything on your plate. Cut your food sufficiently small to eat it comfortably and then when you place the food into your mouth, concentrate on all the tastes and textures. Chew your food correctly and enjoy it. So many illnesses and ailments these days are caused by the rush of our lives. When you take your time and live in the moment while eating, you open up your senses to wonderful treats and also help your health.

Mindful breathing

When you use mindfulness to look at the way that you are breathing, you actually breathe better. This can be used when you are being pulled into an argument to help you to distance yourself from it until you can tackle whatever the problem is with clarity, rather than anger. The more you practice this, the better you will get at it and it helps you so much in life to be calm and able to cope with everything life throws at you.

Mindfulness in General

Being in the moment encourages you to do one task at a time and you are more likely to achieve good results when you do that. Scientists already know that multi-tasking goes against the natural workings of the brain. People who are mindful put everything that they can into the job that they are currently doing. Have you ever watched an old lady knitting? If you have, you probably saw practiced mindfulness at work. She is so absorbed in the moment that she is capable of producing wonderful results with seemingly little effort. When you tackle tasks in your life, no matter how mundane, mindfulness helps you to be grateful to be able to do that job. Believe me, I know what I am saying.

Cleaning floors has never been such a pleasure and the results I get are better than they have ever been before. Why? Because I am in that moment and am giving everything I am to the task at hand.

Every moment of your life gives you an opportunity to be mindful. If you want to see the real power of mindfulness at work, go to one of your favorite places at sunset where the scenery is awe inspiring. When you do, simply sit and think of nothing at all but what surrounds you. The more you practice mindfulness the richer your life becomes. You notice every facet of life right down to the small details and are thus able to celebrate it in a more complete way.

CHAPTER 14: THE BIGGEST OBSTACLE TO MINDFULNBESS

Add cWithout doubt this is the biggest obstical – the "I want something more" attitude.a better question is what excites me?or what sparks joy in me? Want is never ending question..

While we are always striving for achievement, only few are thinking of actual fulfillment. We are all seeing life as two dimensional; nobody is thinking on a three-dimensional basis.

If I get this, then I will be happy.

If I achieve that, then I will be happy.

Nobody is realizing the fact that it's not reaching the mountain top which makes you happy; it is the journey, the persistence and the creativity of the mind while you are walking that will truly make you happy and fulfilled. "It is not the destination, it is the journey." While you have probably heard these words a million times, you need to live it as if you have heard it for the first time.

So how do you attain this non-seeking mindset,(wait don't worry.With this attitude you will do better in the material world too jst relax) which is always happy and fulfilled? That's a great question! It is simply by recognizing those "something more" beliefs when they arise. Recognize them, then and there, for what they are – they are just thoughts. They are not reality, and are not entirely true; they are not something we have to play out, and they are not things that have to induce stress about things which we feel have to 'get done'.

When one of these thoughts arises, just smile at it! Smile at it and drop it! Take three slow breaths, returning your awareness to the present – which is the magnificent miracle of life unfolding right now, in front of you. Don't miss it! By returning to ourselves, we rediscover all the beauty and the love. All of the peace we ever wanted was here all along, if we can only open our eyes to see it.

Chapter 15: How Does Mindfulness Training Benefit Us?

Mind training often called mindfulness training can open many doors in your life. Few people understand how powerful the subconscious in and that you can rewire it to attract wealth, health, and overall well being and access.

With many people under pressure in our fast paced technology filled world more and more are suffering from depression. People do not know what they need for feeling happy and fulfilled.

Millions of people are suffering and being treated for depression all over the world and cases continue to grow.

Through research it has been discovered that mindfulness therapy for depression treatment may be a better more natural way of treating this illness than through anti depressant pills.

The proper way forward to get maximum benefits of mindfulness therapy for depression is learning the arts of meditation, and this can a only be taught through following proper training and guidance from experts.

The case of high expenses for this sort of training can be cut through taking online mindfulness training and meditation courses readily available, and following them through until you have learnt to find natural fulfillment.

If you are feeling depressed it is probably for reasons you realize but do not know how to treat. Perhaps you are feeling unfulfilled, wondering what your life purpose is, and feeling loss, deeply dissatisfied with what life has dealt you, or something deeply hidden in your subconscious.

Consider trying to start from a point with a wonderful training in mindfulness cognitive therapy.

You may find that practicing this correctly will ultimately help you turn your entire life around and get you off anti depressants. Most importantly your entire outlook on your life will change making you realize that every minute you are alive is precious.

The sensible way to learn mindfulness exercises combined with meditation and even Yoga is from the masters.

Mindfulness exercises using meditation and the help of audio can allow you to retrain your mind. Transcendental Meditation can be done anywhere and will produce a deep state of peace calmness and relaxation.

Learning meditation basics is easier with the help of audio. Here are beautiful audio files to help you achieve maximum enjoyment practicing **mindfulness exercises**. (ADVERTISER)

Once you have mastered mind control you can map your life into fulfillment choosing for tranquility, peace and harmony even though the world around you is swirling with fast paced technologies and noise.

Mindfulness exercises will help you eliminate jumbled thoughts and help you concentrate while reducing stress.

The result is enhanced physical and emotional well being.

It is worthwhile investing in meditation videos and music, a course in Yoga, programs in mind training and subconscious management and they will definitely change your life.

Mindfulness exercises come with many life coaching programs because without proper mind training you can be adrift in chaos and disorder. Stress in our daily lives has many additional mental frames of mind that come with it all damaging your inner peace. Aggression, frustration, impatience, and depression can all be caused by stress.

Chapter 16: Walking Mindfulness

This is an exercise for practicing mindfulness as you're walking. Before you begin, you need to prepare a space. Remove your shoes if you can, and find a spot where you can walk about twelve to fourteen steps before you turn around. You also want to be in a place where you know you won't step into a hole or trip over something.

1. Begin by noticing your body's posture as you stand still. Feel the connection of your body with the ground or the floor. Become aware of the surroundings, taking in the smells, sights, sounds, tastes, and

other sensations. Notice any emotions and thoughts and allow them to be. Notice how your arms are at your sides or if you prefer, you can hold your right hand in your left hand at the front, or clasp your hands behind you. Notice your breath as it moves in and out of your body. There is no need to change it, just allow it to be.

2. Now shift your body's weight from the left leg and begin to lift the right foot up. Move it forward, put it back down to the ground. Mindfully shift the weight of the right leg and start to lift the left foot up, put it forward, and place it back on the ground.

3. Continue with this walking mindfully, paying attention to the feelings on the soles of your feet. As every part of your sole from the heel to the toe comes in contact with the ground, feel the sensations it creates. Lift, move, place and repeat. Notice how your body is moving while you walk. Walk with awareness one step at a time.

4. When it's time to turn around, maintain the flow of your mindfulness and start to bring your awareness to the intricate process your body takes in order to turn. Slowly and with an awareness of every motion necessary to turn your body, begin to walk back to where you began the process. One step at a time, lift, move, and place your feet.

5. Find a rhythm that's good for you and suits your balance and body. While you move forward, notice the feeling of your body and notice your head on your shoulders, your hands, arms, trunk, legs, and how they move forward with each step.

6. Be aware of any thoughts that come about and allow them to be. Return your focus to the feeling of walking by lifting, moving and putting your feet down. Notice your breath. Is it moving in a rhythm that fits your pace of walking? There's no need to change your breathing, but you might find that it's changed without you noticing.

7. Keep walking, taking care to notice every tiny movement that's required when you turn around. Practice this for some time.

8. The next time you return to the starting spot, be still. Notice any sensations in your body and bring your awareness to your breath. Notice the stillness when the movement stops. Appreciate the time you spent practicing the mindful walking.

Chapter 17: How Mindfulness Meditation Can Change Your Life

People who practice mindfulness in their lives are able to keep in mind brilliantly (to a certain extent) what inspired them to practice in the first place, as well as the life circumstances and feeling tone that led up to that moment of starting. The emotional topology of the moment of realizing or the moment of beginning that you wish to get in touch with yourself in — are unique and rich for everyone.

The direction for living a more mindful and peaceful life appears to be very simple: let your awareness return repeatedly to whatever it is you are feeling or thinking. In this moment is where all the challenges and questions can begin to be resolved. Mindfulness for Beginners offers insights, welcomes answers, and lessons to help us make that shift, slowly, into a more clear and loving relationship with ourselves and the world.

As time passes, mindfulness brings continuing changes in mood & levels of wellbeing. Scientific studies have confirmed that mindfulness not only prevents you from depression, but also it positively affects the brain patterns underlying everyday stress, anxiety, irritability and depression so that when they take place, they dissolve away easier and more quickly.

Other studies have shown that it improves the immune system and people who practice meditation daily spend fewer days in hospital (for numerous infectious diseases, cancer and heart disease) and consult with their doctors less often. Creativity increases, Memory improves and their reaction times become faster.

Thousands of scientific papers confirm that mindfulness reduces chronic pain & enhances ones physical and mental wellbeing. **Here is list of the benefits of using this technique (especially for beginners):**

Mindfulness improves creativity, emotional intelligence, working memory, reaction speeds and attention span. It enhances the mental & physical stamina and flexibility as well.

With regular meditation sessions, the level of anxiety, depression, stress, irritability and exhaustion all can be decreased to a great extent. Mental & physical stamina increases, reaction times to things become faster & memory improves. People who meditate regularly are more content and happier, and at the same time are less likely to experience psychological distress.

Clinical trials give you an idea that mindfulness helps improving mood & quality of life in tough medical illnesses, which includes cancer, multiple sclerosis and in chronic pain situations such as fibromyalgia (a lot of pain, flu-like feeling, and sleep disruption) and lower back pain.

Mindfulness also helps in chronic functional disorders for instance Irritable Bowel Syndrome (IBS).

Mindfulness can significantly decrease pain and its emotional reaction. Recent trials advise that unpleasantness 'average pain' levels could be reduced by 57% whereas skilled meditators report an overall reduction of up to 93%.

Mindfulness reduces self-destructive and addictive behavior. These include excessive alcohol intake and the abuse of illegal & prescribed drugs.

Mindfulness can be used as treatment for clinical-level depression. The UK's National Institute for Health & Clinical Excellence strongly recommends a structured program also called MBCT (Mindfulness-Based Cognitive Therapy) as one of the preferred treatments.

Mindfulness and Meditation both contribute to improving the control of blood sugar in type 2 diabetes. Meditation lowers the risk of hypertension as well, and it improves heart & circulatory health.

Meditation can help your brain to function in a better way. It improves grey matter in areas linked with self-control & attention, empathy, and self-awareness. It calms the brain parts that create stress hormones and builds those areas that lift mood & encourage learning.

Chapter 18: Zazen Breath Awareness Meditation

Zazen is a type of meditation from the school of Buddhism, but it originated in Japan. A rough translation means 'sitting meditation' since 'za' means sitting, and 'zen' means meditation. Buddhism actually began with meditation practice, in which Buddha achieved enlightenment almost 3,000 years ago. It was the central core of his teaching, but over time, other practices of meditation have been developed, which also included learning of theories and teaching of devotion to ideals and rituals.

The modern definition of Zen has become associated with relaxation, peace, calm demeanor and serenity. It's important to remember that Zen is not a religion in and of itself, nor is it a philosophy. It is more of a way to free the mind and body and is compatible with many religious traditions.

Unlike many other religious rituals, the emphasis is placed more on the direct experience of achieving enlightenment, not on the beliefs or any sacred texts of religions.

As odd as it sounds, when one is practicing sitting or Zazen meditation, they are just sitting there. There is an old saying, 'when the body sits but the mind wanders.' Therefore, Zazen is a wonderful technique to start your journey on meditation.

Our minds are always busy. Even when you try to sit there and think about thinking about nothing, you're still thinking. This is what is known as stimulus-independent-thinking to modern researchers. You may be thinking about what you need to pick up at the grocery store, think about your mother, or other stimuli you are picking up from the environment around you.

Your mind is using this downtime to what it may think is a good use, and there is nothing wrong with that. However, this can become such a powerful habit that we cannot disengage our thought processes when they are not beneficial and that's when the problems related to stress and anxiety may come in. It is also difficult to think about other things, like the smell of a flower, or how blue the sky is when your mind is in overdrive. You can't enjoy the moment when you're always thinking about, or worrying about, other things.

In Zazen, the practitioners focus on their breathing. By doing this, you and your mind are focused on taking air from the outside into the inside of the body. It is, at the very simplest, focusing on the moment.

Take a minute, if you will, and think about all the times during the day you are multi-tasking. You may be throwing a load of laundry into the washer, taking one out of the dryer and talking on your cell phone or texting at the same time. Think of all those neurons firing at once and you can see how time seems to fly by, or memory gets lost somewhere.

One of the main goals of meditation is to live in the moment. Another example could be washing up the supper dishes. While your hands are busy washing a plate, your mind is pushing you to hurry up so you can watch your favorite TV show, have a cup of coffee, or some other activity we are anticipating doing. So, what is lost?

What is lost is the actual washing of the dishes. You don't feel the warmth of the soapy water. You don't appreciate the feel of the China plate. In other words, you are so lost in the future activities you forget to enjoy the task you are currently involved in. I would say 'engaged' in, but are you really? No, because you are too busy thinking of things to come.

Please don't get me wrong. This exercise can be very difficult to master because your mind is always going ninety miles an hour. As adults, we just seem to have so much to do, and so little time to accomplish all this, it is just overwhelming.

Children, on the other hand, know instinctively how to weed out the madness. Think back to when you were a youngster. Think of a day when you woke, no school, no agenda, no job. You went outside and found a nice calm spot, and you sat down. Your mind wasn't on school assignments or chores. You were living in the moment and enjoying just being there.

The legend goes that the founder of Zazen used the example when he developed this breathing center technique. Later in his life, he tried many kinds of meditation, but he returned to this simple method near the end. What a wonderful story!

Think if you will as the exercise is a means to the focus of your awareness. Over time, you will naturally and gradually expand your awareness from a chaotic and isolated focus to one that is broader and helps you to be aware of your thoughts and what causes them.

The Sitting Posture and Why It's so Vital

This is a journey in which sitting meditation will take you through the stages of awareness. The physical posture is important for two reasons: 1) you want to be comfortable, and 2) Zazen is a somatic practice.

'Soma' means experiencing the body from within, not the body in particular. This is a mental experience, so as you are meditating you will first, recognize you are in a calm and safe space. Then, and only then, we tune into the 'moment'. We feel the ground beneath where we are sitting. We hear the birds in the trees, and we feel the air on our faces.

After that, we start within the body where tension is felt. We focus on that tension and relax it. We also find where there is warmth, nervousness, or excitement is located, and give it permission to leave as well.

A five-minute session of Zazen can leave you feeling calm, with clarity, and increased attention that can last up to an hour for some, or a full day for others. This is brought about because your mind releases or decompresses from its usual chaotic, ninety mile an hour activity, and opens to new insights. Zazen is not the only form of meditation that does this.

If all this happens with just one sitting, how do you think your body will react to a long-term practice? How would you like to retrain your mind to see your environment in an entirely new way? Your life will become more balanced, richer and full of meaning. This develops our understanding of the connections to the world in which we live, but also the world that we want to become a reality.

Zen is a fascinating portion of Buddhistic meditation because it brings the picture of monks living high on a mountain top and martial arts. In reality, the monks find contentment, joy, and comfort in the completion of the simplest of tasks, simply because they are living in the moment.

In our modern world, there seems to be a new technological wonder invented every day or two. We are all caught up with all the electronic media, jobs, schedules, families, and a thousand other things to ruin our peace. What will you get from Practicing Zazen Breath Awareness Meditation? Following is a partial list. You may think of others.

Focus

The only task in this type of meditation is to be aware of each and every breath. This will increase your ability to focus your attention like a laser on whatever you choose.

Patience

You may be in a hurry to learn how to be patient, but remember, this will fade as the experience itself becomes more to the forefront. You will have more patience and the feeling of needing to rush to the next level will decrease.

Clarity

You will become more grounded and your breath awareness will help to calm your mind and end that constant self-talk that goes on. In other words, you will Transcend the noise and distractions that surround you.

Mind-Body Connection

The chronic tension of your daily life that ends up in your body will be lessened by focusing attention to the current moment, and the pressure of worries, bills, ambitions, and concerns will lift. Micro changes will begin to happen in your body with every breath you take and let out.

Self-Awareness

You will develop a deeper more fulfilling connection with your own mind, thoughts, and emotions.

Self-regulation

Self-awareness will lead to a more direct idea of your physical and mental reactions to your everyday life and you will feel a lessening of attachments to your feelings and thoughts. By becoming more in touch with the simple feelings and thoughts, you will start to be less harsh in your own self-directed criticisms.

Joy

By learning to appreciate the small simple things in life, you choose to take back your attention, and control, over your own thoughts. You will find joy in a simple task and learn to savor every moment.

Questions:

What areas of your emotional life do you hope to change by doing this mediation? Is it emotional? Mental? Relationships with others?

Enlightenment comes on many levels and in many forms. What is the intended level of enlightenment you are seeking?

Enlightenment also means knowing yourself. Did this meditation change any of the feelings you have toward you? Did you notice a change in the level of self-criticism?

Chapter 19: Before you get started

Targeting your stress requires

It is impossible for human beings to completely eliminate stress but we could considerably reduce its grip in our lives. Part of managing anxiety is expecting when it may appear and thinking up a strategy to take care of it as it does. This is a procedure that involves analyzing stress causes and what works well to help lessen anxiety.

Tactics to capture your nervousness before it strikes:

• Understand your particular symptoms. What are your ideas as soon as your stress dissipates? In what scenarios do your symptoms include?

• Know what functions. Which approaches are especially beneficial in minutes of high stress? Maybe deep breathing or special mindfulness exercises from this novel.

Talking to just being having a service person can assist too.

The next step is to make a strategy for how you are going to control your anxiety the moment it appears. Developing a written program is a fantastic idea since it is something concrete which you may hold in your hands and examine, which also can help commit it to the memory card.

Your strategy might look something like that:

When I begin to detect the anxiety within my own body or mind, I'll do such things.

This is how I'll use mindfulness to decrease my stress at the moment.

If I'm feeling especially unsettled, I'll call or text.

Here is what I shall do daily to maintain a wholesome lifestyle and mind-set so as to keep stress at bay.

Establishing an outlined schedule of just how and when to utilize mindfulness can allow you to remain in charge of your own anxiety. Stress will happen from time to time, however it does not need to dictate your behavior.

Finding what works for you

Mindfulness is a worldwide strategy that may assist everyone to reduce their stress and enhance their well-being but because of everyone experiences pressure otherwise, the approaches for handling your symptoms are individualized and unique to you. To determine what works best, experimentation with the techniques outlined within this book till you locate the appropriate mixture of strategies that helps lower your nervousness and matches your daily life and everyday routine. Here are the initial steps toward bettering your stress management strategy:

Earn a listing. Start off by composing a list of the exercises which resonated with one of the maxima. Maintaining a working list of approaches that work for you in a purse, pub or some other available place can allow you to handle your stress if you are feeling too flustered at the moment to recall what to do with this. A brief, clear collection of carefully selected exercises is far better than a lengthy, less concentrated one.

Earn a schedule. As soon as you have your record, it is important to think of a schedule if you are likely to exercise your workouts on a regular basis. These exercises must become part of your normal routine such as anything, the longer exercise, the longer you are feeling that has the positive aspects. Doing a minimum of one exercise daily until it turns into a habit is your very best method to come up with an empowering regular which finally can change both your connection to stress and your lifetime.

Furthermore, these tips can help you produce and personalize a sustainable mindfulness care program:

Select a time of day to exercise mindfulness. Possessing a normal schedule makes it possible to adhere to it.

Select a setting where you'll possess a comfortable spot to sit down or lie down. Fill out space with decorations, furniture and items that bring you pleasure.

Create your clinic a ritual. Have tea or another calming, non-alcoholic, non-caffeinated drink. Place on soothing, meditative music or maintain the space quiet, whichever you want. Perhaps light a candle or utilize a vital oil diffuser.

Do not limit yourself. If you've got a meeting or another sort of responsibility that blows to the center of your normal mindfulness period, allow yourself to make the required alterations without feeling stressed about it. Normal practice motivates one to create the mindfulness dependence and will go a very long way in reducing stress but it does not signify you need to be stiff.

Find methods to enhance and revel in your practice. Consider it as an enjoyable time instead of a chore or burden. In our hectic, overscheduled lives, taking a rest for reflection and quiet could be a real cure. Recall that your motive for self-improvement: to live an excellent life, free of stress's control. Understanding your goal can allow you to keep motivated to keep routine, consistent exercise.

Locating support

During the exercises, you have infinitely increased chances for a positive shift in your lifetime. You have got the knowledge and expertise to actively lower your nervousness and begin living in the present time. Nonetheless, these lessons bring about new challenges. When you have developed a steady mindfulness regimen, it is not unusual to encounter flares of stress from time to time. These endings are temporary; however they do not necessarily feel temporary whenever they occur. It is necessary to stay aware that they'll pass and also to get a support network of people that you can trust and hope when fear strikes.

Support could take several forms: spirits, trainers, associations and service groups. Find assistance both on the internet and in the actual world you reside in. Not all service systems are ideal for everybody. A few people can take advantage of regular sessions with a therapist whereas many others do better in class settings.

To optimize your odds of staying on the trail, plan to devote some time daily studying and finishing the exercises. Perhaps start with 15 or even 20 minutes daily and fix as required. Make every exercise unique having a cup of coffee or tea or any other small enjoyment.

It is a good thought to have a laptop to utilize your workbook. There are occasions when you are going to want to compose over the distance around the pages of this workbook allows.

Now, you're prepared for the journey in the current moment, so let's begin.

Chapter 20: Recognizing Stress In The Body

Although it is very important to choose activities that give you pleasure, it is also extremely important to pay attention to what happens to your mind and body when you are under stress. Symptoms of stress do move beyond feelings of concern or worry to other physical reactions. Therefore, it is important to learn how to cope with it.

Mindfulness doesn't get rid of stress and anxiety. It helps work differently with it.

It is important to mention that stress is normal. Stress is the body's reaction to harmful situations, whether they are real or perceived. You find stress at work, in the family, on the road. Stress is everywhere. A little stress is OK and it might be beneficial to make you move and don't live in indolence. Too much stress, however, can make you sick both physically and mentally. Too much stress is harmful for the health. When you feel threatened, chemical reactions occur in your body. These allow you to act to prevent injury. These reactions are known as "fight-or-flight," or the stress response, and get you ready to act. It is how you protect yourself. Although these defense mechanisms are necessary, experiencing them often will cause harm to the health in the long term. Therefore, it is very important to recognize when you are under stress, to leave the autopilot, and become aware of what is happening within yourself.

The first step to controlling stress is to recognize it, to know its symptoms. Most people are so used to be stressed all the time that they often don't know they are actually stressed until they are at breaking point.

 Think Carefully About This

How do you recognize stress in the body?

What happens physiologically when you are under stress?

When you are under threat, your heart rate increases, your breathing quickens, your muscles tighten, and your blood pressure increases. Let's see what actually causes these reactions.

When you are stressed, feeling threatened, and you feel the butterflies in the stomach, what causes these butterflies?

It's the exit of blood from the stomach. When you are under threat, for survival, you take the blood from the stomach to the legs and the arms, either to run away or to fight. So when you have a threat - and any stress is a threat - you can get butterflies, because you have a fight-or-flight response. That is the blood leaving the stomach to go to the limbs.

Do you know what happens physiologically to the eyes when you have a threat?

You maximize your sight, so the pupils open and the eyes widen, and if you have a lot of stress you can have tension around the eyes because they are much wider than they should be.

Do you know why you get a headache?

When you have any kind of stress, even if it's low stress, the heart beats faster so that you get blood to the lungs and to the legs and arms, either to run away or to fight. If you have more blood pumping the pressure goes up and you get headaches.

Do you know why you lose your short-term memory when you have stress?

There is one very important thing that happens when you have a threat, which is the release of adrenaline. Adrenaline makes you feel like superman. You feel like you could do anything. However, at the same time, you have another chemical release, which is called cortisol. Cortisol has the effect of reducing inflammation and protecting the physiology of the body, but in the brain it suppresses the prefrontal cortex. It suppresses the ability to make clear decisions. The technical term for it is "Executive Function". It suppresses the executive function for 3 to 5 minutes when you have a stress.

When I say stress, it could be caused by any threat, such as having negative thoughts, being judged by someone, or being in a dangerous situation. When you are faced by a tiger you don't want to know whether it is a big or a small tiger. You don't want to know whether it is a hungry tiger or a non-hungry tiger. When a bus comes against you in the street, you don't want to know whether it is a slow bus or a fast bus. No, you just jump! As well as situations that put your life in danger, all judgements, anger, and negative thoughts are threats. This is an ancient system in your brain, in the limbic system, which is the system where your emotional life is largely housed.

Take this example. Cats and Zebras don't get ulcers. Why not?

Cats and Zebras don't get ulcers because they don't think about the threat. They don't go away and think about it all day long and all night long. They just lie down on the grass, they sleep and they carry on with their lives. Human beings don't do that. Human beings keep thinking about the stress. If someone has been horrible to us at work or in the family we might think about that one argument a hundred times a day. The cat just has one fight and he falls asleep. Human beings have one argument and they think about it for days, months, or years. This is why we get ulcers, stress, and illness. It is because we can't let go of the threat.

 Think Carefully About This

What do you think you can you do to respond to stress rather than react?

Exercise – 3-Minute Breathing Space

In mindfulness there's a short but very effective exercise to help you cope with stress. It is called the 3-minute breathing space. Of course every person may find his/her own way or strategy to cope with stress, but the 3-minute breathing space - sometimes also called the 3-step breathing space - can be what you can do if you want to respond to stress rather than react and keep it going.

If you want to be like the zebra and the cat you can do the 3-minute breathing space because it stops thinking from getting worse. It helps you come back to a clear perspective and then you might decide to do something about the situation. It's not meant to stop your stress. It's just meant to bring you back to a level ground where your brain is operating in an optimum way, where cortisol has reduced to a point that you can think clearly again.

Of course you will not do the 3-minute breathing space if you are faced by a tiger or a bus, but it is very effective when you feel a difficult situation is coming, when you have an argument with someone, or when you feel nervous before an event.

Guidance for Posture and Comfort

You start the 3-minute breathing space by stopping what you are doing and finding a calm place to sit. If you are at home, you can go to your bedroom or any other place where you feel comfortable, and stop what you are doing. If you are at work, you have to find a place where you can be on your own and no one will disturb you. Probably the bathroom. It doesn't matter, as long as you can find some peace.

Begin the exercise by inviting a dignified posture. A posture that is a signal to yourself that you are about to take some action to look after yourself.

Practice while you read. After you read and learn this exercise, start practicing with your eyes closed.

First minute - Check in with your body.

For the first minute you check in with your body, inviting an awareness of your inner experience. Notice your experience from the inside.

Notice the thoughts. Realize if you have any thoughts or if your mind is simply a bit of a blank. Don't struggle to find the thoughts. Just acknowledge them as they arise.

Notice the feelings. Perceive the feelings you have right now. Tune in as best you can to emotions or mood. Acknowledge the presence of different emotions or maybe the relative absence of them. With an open heart just notice what is there.

Notice the body sensations. Notice the temperature of the body, areas of relaxation or tension, or just a general sense of the shape of your body in this very moment. There is no need to change anything. Just notice whatever is there.

Second minute – Breath.

For the second minute you move your attention very clearly to your breath and, if possible, the breath moving in your body. Place your hand on the belly or the chest, and pick up the movement as the breath flows in and out.

Bring your full attention to the breath movements right now. Is the inhale shorter or longer than the exhale? Is the breath shallow or deep? Sense that wave-like motion, the pattern of the breath moving in and out of the body. When you notice the mind has wandered as it probably will, bring it directly back, pick up the next movement, the next breath, and go on with the practice.

Third minute – Expanding out.

For the third minute, gently expand your attention outwards to the whole body and the environment around you. Feel the parts of the body that touch the ground. The way the arms hang from the shoulders, the balance of the head, and the expression your face might be holding in this moment. Gently notice the whole of your body experience.

Finally, beyond the body, sense the temperature of the air and the sounds around. Sounds from the near environment. Open yourself to a general sense of the space that you're in. The world surrounding you as you breathe in and breathe out. Open yourself to that connection with the space around you. Gently, as best you can, invite the awareness from this practice into the next moments of your day.

If you have already learned how to do the 3-minute breathing space and have started to practice it with your eyes closed, when you finish it, gently prepare yourself to come back to your awareness, by smoothly opening your eyes, looking to the ground, and then looking in front.

3-Minute Breathing Space Exercise Summary

Mind the posture

First Minute – Internal experience. Notice thoughts, feelings, and sensations.

Second Minute – Notice the breath. Acknowledge the breath movements in the body.

Third Minute – External experience. Expand your attention to the environment around.

Tips to Remember!

- You can do this exercise as often as needed. It can be done quickly if you practice regularly.

- Don't judge what you are doing and how you are feeling. Just take the experience as it is.

- Acknowledge when you become distracted by the thoughts and come back to the senses.

 Self-Reflection

How was this practice for you?

How do you feel after this exercise?

How do you feel the 3-minute breathing space can help you in your daily life?

You can do this exercise anytime of the day, at home, at work, when you wake up, when you have a difficult communication with someone. This is an effective and quick exercise to check in with yourself and help you not to react to the situation but to respond by taking better decisions.

Mindfulness can be done very quickly when you practice it. When you do your practice it is available in these moments, when normally you would react. It can come to your rescue when you want to react.

I encourage you to see what happens if you bring a bit of awareness to moments when you feel a difficult communication starting and see what happens, and also to check within yourself what patterns of communication you have. It can be very interesting and quite challenging.

Chapter 21: The Body Scan Technique

The body scan practice is also one of the more popular forms of mindfulness commonly practiced in hospitals and rehabilitation centers. This technique establishes a stronger mind-body connection. This will help you become more alert, and yet you will feel more relaxed.

You can practice this technique while lying down, but if you're sitting, try to maintain a straight back. So, to begin, place both of your hands on your thighs. Relax your shoulders and then close your eyes. Place your arms on your side. Do not slouch. If you're lying down, keep your back straight.

Take a few deep breaths. Inhale through your nose and exhale through your mouth. Breathe high into your nostrils and try to expand your chest and then release your breath through your mouth. Observe your chest rising and dropping each time you take a breath. Pay attention to the sound of your breath. Do this around 20 times to get your mind and body in a relaxed state. Pay attention to your breath. Is it fast? Is it slow?

Now, try to let go of any tension in your body. Try to breathe out all the tension in your body as you exhale. Just stay still and pay attention to your breathing.

Now, shift your attention from your breath to your forehead and to the top of your head. Do you feel any discomfort in your head and forehead? Notice any sensations in that area of your body. Do you feel a tingling sensation on your head? Does it feel hot or cool? Can you feel any tension? Does it feel itchy? Just take time to notice these sensations.

Then, shift your attention to the back of your head. Do you feel an itch on the back of your head? Do you feel any tension? What are the sensations that you feel?

Move your attention to your neck. Take time to notice the skin on your neck. Notice any itching or burning sensation in your neck. Do you feel some tension in that area of your body?

Then, shift your attention to your shoulder. Do you notice any tension or ache? What are the sensations that you feel in your shoulders? Notice how your shoulder moves as you inhale and exhale.

Bring your attention to your arms. Take time to notice each arm. Notice any pain or ache in that region of your body. Do you feel muscle spasms? Do you feel burning sensations in your arms?

Draw your attention to your left elbow and take time to notice the skin on your elbow? Is it dark? Take time to examine the lines on your elbow. Do you feel any sensation on your elbow? Do you feel any tension? Then, shift your attention to your wrists and then to your hands. Pay attention to each finger. Feel the deep muscles in your hands.

Then, notice your back. Watch the movement of your back as you breathe. Then, move your attention to your buttocks. Give your buttocks your full attention even for a moment. Then, move your awareness to your pelvis and then to the muscle of your thighs. Pay attention to those muscles. Do you feel any sensation? Is it relaxed? Do you feel any tension or pain on your thighs?

Then, take time to notice your knees. Bring your full attention to each knee and then move your gaze to your calves. Do you feel any tension on your calves? Do they feel heavy? Notice any pain and then move your full attention to your feet. Do you feel any burning sensation or itchiness on your feet? Take time to notice the contact of your soles to the ground. Does it feel cold or warm? If you're wearing shoes, are your shoes loose or tight?

Turn your attention to your whole body. How does your body feel? Do you feel good about your body? Are you experiencing any pain or tension? Then, bring your focus back to your breath. Pay attention to how your chest rises and collapses as you breathe. During this process, distracting thoughts will enter your mind – trivial thoughts, thoughts of better days, and even worries. When this happens, simply acknowledge those thoughts and then let those thoughts go. Bring your focus back to your breath. Bring your focus back to the present moment.

To improve your cognitive function and health, it is important that you do this exercise on a daily basis. Do this exercise for 3-10 minutes daily, and in just a few weeks, you'll see amazing results. You'll feel healthier, happier, and more alive.

Chapter 22: A Mindful Body

Your body records and expresses everything your mind feels. The majority of human communication is nonverbal ("What Are the 9 Types of Nonverbal Communication You Might Be Missing," 2019). This is something we all know and understand. How many times have you formed an impression of someone without them saying a word? How many times has your intuition been correct?

If the body expresses what the mind feels, can changing your body awareness affect your mind? The answer is a resounding yes! Your mind and body are connected and feedback flows both ways. So, utilizing mindfulness techniques to influence the way your body moves will have excellent implications for reducing your stress.

Body Awareness

When talking of meditation, a lot of beginners to the practice start fantasizing of having an out of body experience. Reality is far more anticlimactic. Meditation is a deeply "in the body" experience and, if anything, you get far closer to it. If you want an out of body experience, you only need to open your eyes and look at how you usually live.

We constantly travel between the past and the future, loaded with worry and pain. We fret about our future and worry about our past. We regret decisions made and fantasize about correcting them. We envision futures where all our problems vanish and we're in bliss. All the while, the present lies there ignored and unattended. What is this if not an out of body experience?

Being present is being deeply connected to your body in the moment and truly experiencing everything that is going on with it. It is to explore it and see where knots exist and where certain aches and pains exist. Where do pleasant sensations exist and so on. The thing is that not all of the stuff your mind communicates to you come to you as words or emotions ("What Are the 9 Types of Nonverbal Communication You Might Be Missing," 2019).

They manifest as physical sensations and once you bring awareness to them, you'll unearth what your mind is telling you. At the end of this chapter you will receive a full body meditation technique which will help you immensely when it comes to developing greater body awareness.

For now, you can take a moment to travel inwards and spend time within your body to see how certain body parts feel. Something must be in pain or sore somewhere. Don't judge this, but marvel at how easy it is to disconnect from your body and pay no heed to it.

Some people have trouble exploring their body from a mindful perspective and think that they need to change the way their body moves. This is not what I'm talking about. Much like how you explore your mind, you need to explore your body using the eight pillars of mindfulness.

This means that even if some portion of your body is hurting, you remain still and acknowledge it and observe it. You don't need to torture yourself, like some ancient Indian sages used to do, but don't go to the other extreme and aim to get as comfortable as possible.

Dealing With Pain

Pain is quite literally a painful topic to deal with and we have powerful inbuilt mechanisms to deal with it. There are two types of pain that you need to be aware of. The first is acute pain which cannot be cured through mindfulness. This is the pain that results from a physical injury or a problem that has occurred in your life. Pain of this kind needs a medical solution and not a spiritual one.

The second kind of pain is chronic pain. The origin of chronic pain may be physical but there is a huge emotional and cognitive component to it which mindfulness can address. While the elimination of pain is a stretch, reducing the burden you carry as a result of it is certainly possible. Research shows that meditation and other mindfulness practices can help address chronic pain (Penman, 2019).

While meditation by itself is very effective, applying an entire framework of mindfulness to the issue is a better approach. So, how do you do this? Well, the first step is to begin by investigating the pain.

Step One

The common reaction we have to pain is to clench our muscles around the area that causes pain and then deeply wish it goes away. In short, our reaction has both a physical and emotional component to it and in the throes of pain it is difficult to separate the two. Mindfulness will allow you to do just that.

Why is it important to separate the two parts of your reaction? Well, for one thing your emotions to the pain often makes it far worse than it really is. Think of a child who falls to the ground when she thinks no one is watching. More often than not, the child will dust themselves off and keep running. However, when the child senses her parents are watching and as she sees the looks of concern as they rush towards her, she will inevitably start crying.

In this case, the negative emotions of the parents lead the child to believe her pain is far worse than it actually is. Most of the pain is just plain emotional exaggeration though. A similar thing happens to us as adults as well, even if we don't shed tears. This heightened emotion causes us to react physically to the pain in inappropriate ways as well.

While clenching muscles around the painful area is a normal reaction, you'll find when performing your body scan practice that the extent of this clenching goes far beyond just the affected area. Clenching your muscles to this extent communicates a stress response to your brain and it accordingly executes what it needs to.

A stress response is your body's mechanism of dealing with mortal threats. When your brain detects a mortal threat, it redirects blood flow to your limbs, prioritizes certain bodily functions, such as physical movement and respiration to enable a quick flight, and deprioritizes others, such as digestion. All of this puts tremendous stress on your body. Adrenaline is secreted, which gives you an additional boost and makes you temporarily immune to pain.

This state of affairs cannot last for long because it puts a huge load on your internal organs and functions. If you spend too much time in such situations, your brain will simply shut down and demand rest. Prolonged exposure will result in traumas like PTSD and so on. While the stress you feel might not be of the same degree as a mortal threat, its very presence puts strain on your body.

This is why by relaxing your body, you can remove the stressful interpretation of events your brain is currently stuck processing. The practice at the end of this chapter will show you how to release the tension that accompanies pain. Another way mindfulness recommends is to ride the pain and notice how it ebbs and flows.

Impermanence is a central concept in mindfulness and by noticing how your pain throbs, you realize that it isn't a constant thing and that it is simply another vibration in your body.

Step Two

Should you suffer when you feel pain? Think about that question a little bit more before thinking of an answer. You see, pain and suffering are two different things. Pain is what the stimulus is. Suffering is born out of your reaction to the pain. So, with this in mind, ask yourself is it necessary to suffer when you feel pain?

The simple answer is no, it isn't. In reality though, it is difficult to live this way. We're used to blending our suffering together with our experience of pain so that it forms one seamless reaction. Mindfulness will teach you to separate the two. The first thing to examine is whether you have any resistance to allowing your emotions to flow.

We're taught a lot of things about exhibiting our emotions, ranging from presenting a stoic outlook towards things to flat out denying the validity of the ones we feel. General wisdom is to acknowledge emotions and let them be. This is unfortunately not enough.

Acknowledgement must be accompanied by acceptance if it is to be useful. Mere acknowledgement is simply recognizing that emotions exist but doesn't imply engagement with them. Similarly, to let your emotions be is to give them some space to exist but not engage with them anymore.

You need to accept and let your emotions pass through you. The key to doing this is to understand your choice with regards to responding to those emotions. By observing and striving to maintain equanimity, you improve your ability to deal with pain and detach the emotional response from the stimulus.

Hence, you will be free to feel the pain, but you need not compound your suffering by reacting inappropriately to it.

Step Three

The third and most important step is to set your intention to live in the present moment. Deal only with what is making itself known to you right now and don't worry about what it means for the future. If you're experiencing pain in this moment, then deal with it now. If it presents itself in the next moment, deal with it then.

As an example, if you bump your head on something pretty badly, experience the pain and feel the negative emotion welling up inside you. It hurts and your emotions are valid. Don't bottle them up. Try to separate the physical sensation from your emotional reaction but if you can't do this, don't worry about it.

You might be worried if you're bleeding. Well, check to see if you are. Worrying about whether you're bleeding and then thinking you will need to go to the hospital and get yourself checked out and then worrying about how much money that's going to cost you and the amount of time you'll need to spend doing this is simply compounding your suffering.

It is also travelling into the future to see what might happen. Mindfulness requires you to stay in the present and see what happens. Feel your pain and let your emotions through. Once that's done, get back to what you were doing and be on your way. As long as the pain expresses itself, feel it and learn to love it. This is a part of living after all and you cannot have pleasure without pain. So, accept it and allow it to move through you.

Barriers

It is a good idea to examine your thoughts and reactions for any barriers to emotional expression. All of us grow up with certain notions of emotional expression and the thing is that you cannot make emotions disappear by simply denying them expression. They will always manifest themselves somewhere in your body.

If you grew up in a household where no one ever expressed anger or treated anger as an invalid emotion, chances are you have lots of pent up anger stored in your body. How this manifests within you depends from person to person. Some people might feel it as constriction in the chest, others might feel tension in their backs, yet others might feel it as heat in their limbs and so on. When you begin to implement the body scanning practice at the end of this chapter, watch out for signs of emotional constriction or denial.

Another way people deny themselves emotional expression is to confuse thoughts with emotions. For example, if you make a statement such as "I feel useless" or "I feel idiotic," you're confusing your thoughts with your emotions. Words such as "useless" and "idiotic," aside from being negative words you should never use about yourself, happen to be thoughts.

What are the emotions associated with these words? Probably anxiety, fear and so on. Dig through your self-talk and check whether you're bottling your emotions up in the name of giving freedom to your thoughts.

Identifying Emotions

This is a mini practice you can carry out when you feel overwhelmed or whenever the mood strikes you. Write down a bunch of emotions on a piece of paper, such as anxiety, sadness, happiness, love, hate and so on, and think back to moments in your life when you experienced them.

Close your eyes and visualize the pictures that were a part of that incident and place yourself in that point in time again. Now, scan your body to see what you feel. Is there tightness or lightness somewhere? Work with one emotion at a time and journal everything you feel. Note down any supplemental thoughts that make themselves known as well.

You need not analyze all of these thoughts, but over time you'll notice pattern in them, and this will give you clues as to how your mind works.

The Body Scan

To begin this practice, place yourself in a comfortable position, either on the floor or a chair and make sure your spine is not supported. Relax into your environment by taking a few deep breaths and gently closing your eyes. Notice any sounds or ambient noise in your environment and become aware of your presence in this place, at this moment. Feel the extremities of your body and notice how heavy and solid it feels.

Now, bring your awareness to your breath. Notice its characteristics, whether it's hot or cold, and notice how you can relax your body on exhalation. If your mind wanders, let it do so. Once you've become aware of it, bring it gently back to your breath and keep observing how your breath travels in and out.

Now, gently shift your awareness away from your breath to the top of your head. Linger there for a while and focus your awareness on just this area. If any other sensation from a different portion of your body makes itself known, acknowledge it and then get back to the top of your head. If you feel any sensation here, observe it and move on with equanimity.

Do not judge or attach labels to any sensation you feel. Simply observe and move on. Keep moving along the top of your head down to your forehead. Scan your forehead, either in parts or as a whole, for any sensations. Do you feel and tension along the top of your eyebrows? Can you relax it? If you can't, this is not a problem, simply observe how the tension feels.

Does it throb or pulse in any way? Observe this for a few seconds and then move on. Adopt the beginner's attitude throughout the process and be a keen explorer of what is going on with your body. Move to each part of your body, little by little, piece by piece, and observe.

Do not pass judgement on anything or label anything. Remain equanimous and either relax any tension you find or observe it. If you observe pain anywhere or numbness, observe it and see if you're feeling any emotions along with it. Throughout the process observe your emotions.

What sort of thoughts come floating into your head? If one of these thoughts cause your mind to wander, bring your awareness back to where you were. Keep moving through your body and perform as many scans as you can for at least thirty minutes every day at a stretch.

Once you're done or your time is up, gently open your eyes and notice how you feel. Notice if you feel any different or if you feel the same. Do you feel worse? Journal all of this and also jot down any observations that stuck with you as you completed your session.

You can increase the number of sessions or the time spent performing your body scan. The key to the practice is to establish your intent to be equanimous to anything. Observe everything yet attach yourself to nothing. Journal what you feel afterwards and over time, you'll notice certain patterns in this. You'll also notice some areas of your body contain far more stress than others.

All the while, keep observing and don't judge anything.

Chapter 23: The Health Benefits of Mindfulness

You already have an idea of what mindfulness is doing to your body. Your pulse rate will go down, and your lungs will take in more air, which helps to regulate the sympathetic nervous system and even out any imbalance in the amount of oxygen circulating in your blood. You may also be aware that when you panic about something, you breathe in too much air, which is why traditional methods would be to breathe into a paper bag to bring down the oxygen levels and try to normalize the calm in your body.

There are many benefits to mindfulness meditation because what you are doing is clearing out the clutter. Imagine a room filled so full of boxes that you can't move in it. That's a little like the average mind. We see an epidemic of stress because of the world that we live in, and it is known, and mindfulness meditation helps to stem anxiety and is even being prescribed by doctors in the UK as an alternative to traditional medications. The Dalai Lama has written an interesting book that shows the discourse between the medical field and himself in which it can be clearly seen that scientists and doctors are taking the subject very seriously. The fact is that long term, the medications that are currently prescribed don't actually solve the approach of the patient toward their life and thus don't deal with the stress that is becoming a part of their lives. What happens is that they mask the symptoms, and when people come off these medications, they find that repeated treatment is often called for. With mindfulness, it changes the way that people approach life and thus changes the outcome and lessens the stress simply because people are learning new life habits.

Let's look at some other ways in which mindfulness helps the health factor.

Mindfulness helps your brain to function in a better manner, meaning that you will no longer go through the stress that many succumb to in their day-to-day lives because your brain is working without brain fog. Your immune system is able to work better, too, meaning that you can fight off illness, which increases your productivity. Your blood pressure is lowered, which may be good news to those suffering from high blood pressure and, thus, the risk of stroke or heart conditions.

Mindfulness helps those with chronic illness to cope better with pain and also helps those patients suffering from cancer to recover better, due to the fact that they are able to look beyond the worries of cancer and approach the illness in a more positive frame of mind. It can shorten recovery time because the body is better able to bounce back after illness. The biggest decrease that you may expect is that of the incidence of depression, which is addressed in a more efficient way so that the individual is better skilled at dealing with problems of this nature and is less likely to go through repetition of depression as is normal with those on standard medication.

Your general health is improved by the practice of mindfulness meditation, and there is a very logical reason for this. You are taught to look after your body and to listen to intuition more. You are, therefore, less likely to be satisfied with foods that are not particularly good for your body and will no doubt take more exercise and care for your body more than those who do not practice mindfulness. You are mindful of the messages that your brain is sending to different parts of the body and will respect posture, and be less likely to suffer from the effects of it and the stiffness that ensues from bad posture.

Conclusion

Change may not happen as often as quickly as you would like, but as long as you keep persisting, it will come about eventually. Making it through this book means you've done something wonderful today. You've decided to take an active role in looking after your health and wellbeing by learning to better manage your stress. It's a decision that is going to change your life and your health for the better.

Life is short. **Too short** to waste precious seconds of it on anything that doesn't fill your life with joy. **Mindfulness for Stress Management** is here to serve as a reminder. A reminder to be grateful for everything you have. A reminder that every day is a blessing. A reminder that by raising your awareness and mindfully engaging in all aspects of your life, you will come to the realization there are so many wonderful moments you end up missing when you allow stress to rule your day.

Make mindfulness meditation a daily practice. Be mindful in general every chance you get until it eventually becomes a habit to be mindful throughout the day. The present is where you live your life to its fullest potential, not in the past and not in the future.

www.ingramcontent.com/pod-product-compliance
Lightning Source LLC
Chambersburg PA
CBHW072013070526
44583CB00015B/1469